ISBN 978-1-5281-7414-5
PIBN 10101317

ESSAYS

ON

SECONDARY EDUCATION

BY VARIOUS CONTRIBUTORS

.

EDITED BY

CHRISTOPHER COOKSON, M.A.

Fellow and Tutor of Magdalen College, Oxford
Formerly Assistant Master in St. Paul's School

OXFORD

AT THE CLARENDON PRESS

MDCCCXCVIII

· Oxford

PRINTED AT THE CLARENDON PRESS
BY HORACE HART, M.A.
PRINTER TO THE UNIVERSITY

PRELIMINARY NOTICE

THE following essays have one feature in common, that they are the work of men of considerable practical experience, whether as teachers or examiners. It is hoped that under these circumstances the purely academic point of view has been avoided.

But there has been no attempt consistently to maintain any other point of view. Each contributor has written as his own experience suggested. Where therefore any two agree together, their recommendation has at least the force of an identical conclusion independently attained; where they differ, the fact may perhaps strengthen the argument that there is no one method of education applicable to all cases.

The Editor wishes to express his thanks to Mr. H. T. Gerrans, Fellow and Tutor of Worcester College, and one of the Delegates of the Clarendon Press, for much assistance and advice in the preparation of the volume.

TABLE OF CONTENTS

—— ✦ ——

SECONDARY EDUCATION

—+—

SOME DIFFICULTIES OF DAY SCHOOLS

THE Greek poet says that the streams of joy and trouble flow in different ways, and this is as true of day schools as it was of ancient rulers. There are many different kinds of schools which fall under the general head of day schools, and their advantages and difficulties are not in all cases the same. There are, for instance, the Public Secondary Schools, whether old endowed foundations or more recently established by Town and County Councils; there are Proprietary Schools, such as have been founded by public companies or other bodies; and there are Private Schools. All these schools belong to the sphere of secondary education. Then, again, there are the Higher Grade Board Schools, which in some large towns must certainly be considered as giving instruction beyond elementary standards; and lastly, there are the Technical Schools.

I do not propose to deal with the educational

B

difficulties which all these several classes of schools are called upon to meet. Such a task would be beyond the compass of a short paper, and also beyond the reach of my experience. The Director of Special Inquiries in an Education Department is no doubt in a position to compare the experience of many different kinds of schools. The schoolmaster who is practically engaged in teaching has a more limited sphere of opportunity, and what he says will only have a value in being the genuine fruit of his own experience. I propose then to consider only some of the problems and difficulties which have to be faced in the management of those Grammar and High Schools which are either wholly or mainly composed of day boys. Such schools are situated in large towns, for the country grammar schools only to a limited extent consist of day boys, and depend for the most part upon their boarders. Now, although many leading characteristics of day schools are the same for all parts of the country, yet there are features of dissimilarity; for instance, between schools in the north and schools in the south of England, between schools which charge a high fee and schools which charge a low fee, between one of the great London day schools and a day school in a manufacturing town where the professional classes are in a minority. I shall therefore probably lay stress upon some difficulties which are not universally felt in the same degree, and pass over some which weigh more heavily upon other schoolmasters.

The relative merits of day and boarding schools have often been and still are discussed, and some points of difference are mentioned in another paper in this volume. But one practical question of importance which arises out of the difference deserves special emphasis—the question of home-work. The amount of work to be prepared by the boys for the five hours' teaching of a school day is probably much the same in both kinds of school. The conditions under which it is done are different. In the boarding school there are the house-master and the tutor to take note of the amount of the work to be prepared, to give proper help where necessary, and to warn any master who is setting more or less than he should. In a day school, at the end of the teaching day, boys and masters separate, and the boys do their work in preparation for the next day under the varying conditions of their own homes. Some boys are slow, others are quick ; some get help and others get none ; in most cases parents see that the boys have time and opportunity for preparation, in a few cases no such provision is made. If matters are left to take their own course, the masters in each different subject exact all the home-work that they can, whether for languages, mathematics, drawing or other lessons, and the boy is either overtasked or elects to work for the particular master who can apply most pressure. It is necessary that some one master should be responsible for the incidence of the home-work in different subjects in each of the forms into which the school is divided, in order to ensure that on no single night is there an unreasonable amount. This can best be done by careful inquiry by the form-master at the beginning of each term. An average should be taken, and allowance made for the slow or backward. For this purpose it is well occasionally to give opportunity in the class-room for the preparation of work, in order that the master may realize the amount of time which each lesson requires. For the benefit of the parents the school rules should state the average time required for the home-work in different parts of the school, and where the time spent by the boy exceeds or falls short of this amount, the parent should complain. Where these conditions are fulfilled, the difficulties of home-work should be removed. But as boys, masters, and parents are all human, the difficulties are not always removed. Ambitious boys do more than they ought and are not checked by their parents, idle boys are to be found in all schools, and masters are not always sufficiently considerate. To many parents it appears that the proper remedy against excessive home-work is to shorten the holidays. But both for masters and boys the break in school-work given by the present system appears to be necessary. In spite of his holidays the schoolmaster's, if not the schoolboy's, life would seem to be a wearing one. At the age when statesmen have sown their political wild oats, and barristers and medical men are beginning to gain a solid reputation, the schoolmaster is compelled to think of laying himself upon the shelf. A proper understanding between masters and parents is all that is required for the rectification of the difficulty.

Before dealing further with the internal difficulties which are peculiar to day schools, it is necessary to speak of those external conditions which may affect their work. Recent educational reports have shown the difficulties under which some of the smaller grammar schools labour. The head-master of a Board school has the School Board with the purse of Fortunatus to draw upon, — good buildings, adequate apparatus, and trained teachers. The head-master of a small endowed school may sometimes have old-fashioned buildings, prehistoric apparatus, and an insufficient staff; and these are not the conditions of a satisfactory secondary school. The question of ways and means affects all schools, and it is necessary to consider the external conditions under which day schools have to carry on their work.

Endowed schools are for the most part subject to the control of the Charity Commission, which frames schemes prescribing the limit of age for the pupils and the scope of the education to be given in the school. According to the received terminology adopted by the different Parliamentary Commissions, schools are distinguished as first, second, and third grade. First grade schools, with which we are more immediately concerned, are schools which aim at giving an education suitable as a preparation for the so-called learned professions, such as the ministry, law, medicine, teaching in all its branches, literature and science, the Civil Service, and the like. In such schools education is continued till the age of eighteen or nineteen years, and would naturally end in the Universities. The function of the second grade school is education with a view to some form of commercial or industrial life, and types of schools of this kind would be found in the Grammar Schools of Birmingham, the Science Schools of some School Boards, and Municipal Technical Schools. Now even in dealing with first grade schools this second grade education, as it is called, must be considered, because a large day school, with its Classical, Modern, and Science sides, comprises both first and second grade education. Third grade schools—with which we are not here concerned except in so far as they serve the purpose of preparatory schools to the higher education—train boys for the higher handicrafts or the commerce of the shop or town. Such schools are to be found in the Higher Grade Board Schools, which carry on to its completion the primary school course.

Schools however cannot be divided simply according to the character of the instruction given. Social feelings complicate the cut-and-dried systems of educational reformers. If all classes of children attended the same schools, there would be no difficulty in a classification based upon the nature of the education given in each school. As a matter of fact, some large day schools have practically to provide all three kinds of education recognized by the authorities. The classical side represents the first grade school; the upper part of the modern side represents the second grade school, where the education closes at about seventeen, while the lower part of a modern side is often not very different from a third grade school, which boys leave at an early age to pass to the business of the warehouse, factory or bank, with attainments which, from the schoolmaster's point of view, constitute only a slender equipment.

Where the endowment of a school is small or non-existent, and where the school is not able to charge high fees because of the character of the population, it is often compelled to resort to a source of income which brings it under the control of another public authority, the Science and Art Department. In order to obtain the grants which are distributed by this Department, many secondary schools have either formed Science and Art classes according to the regulations of the Department, or have become 'Organized Science Schools,' or 'Schools of Science' as they are now termed in the new Directory—that is, have put the whole or a part of the school under the control of the Department as to courses of instruction and the hours allotted to different subjects. At the outset South Kensington was intended to encourage special subjects likely to be of use for arts and industries, and the examinations were intended for adults; but the use which has been made of the grants has converted the Department into an authority directly or indirectly controlling the education given in secondary schools. *De jure* in some cases, *de facto* in others, it prescribes the subjects taught and the scheme of instruction, fixes the school routine, examines and inspects at its own pleasure, and elaborates intricate and harassing regulations. About these regulations there has been no sort of fixity. From year to year no one knows what surprise the next Directory will have in store. The Education Department has to lay its codes, the Charity Commission has to lay its schemes, upon the table of the House of Commons; but the Science and Art Department seems to be responsible to none but itself for any changes it may see fit to make. The Department does not take into account the character of the institutions which it aids. Whether a school is secondary, or whether it is higher grade elementary, it is in the eyes of the Department a 'School of Science,' or a place where Science and Art classes are held, and must conform to the same conditions in order to earn the grant. The crowd of applicants for these grants is increasing, and the Department seeks to defend itself against increased expenditure by more exacting regulations. It is, in fact, a secular strife between the hardness of the donkey's mouth and the spikes of the thistles— between the Department's powers of resistance and the pertinacity of the applicants for the dole. Many secondary schools are in need of these grants; but

the uncertainty, the irritating nature of the requirements and restrictions, the variability of the standards
of examination, are a source of perpetual trouble in
the management of schools, and must have led many
a schoolmaster to exclaim with the apothecary in
Romeo and Juliet, 'My poverty but not my will
consents.'

Apart from the central authorities already mentioned, other external influences to which a local
school is subject come from the locality itself. Under
recent legislation Town and County Councils have
become educational authorities, entering into various
relations with existing schools as well as establishing
new ones. These bodies do not to any great extent
assist secondary day schools of the kind with which
we are chiefly concerned. For the most part, in their
efforts to promote education they have overlooked
the grammar schools, in some cases because they are
out of sympathy with them, in others because they
do not feel themselves able to help them. The
practice however varies in different parts of the country. Those Town or County Councils which give any
assistance naturally exercise some control. If they
grant scholarships, the scholars must pursue a course
of education which the Councils approve; if they
make grants, they must be satisfied that the money is
properly applied; but so far as my own experience
goes, this control is exercised without undue interference with the management of the school.

Passing now to internal difficulties, we can first

consider the educational material with which day
schools are required to deal. The ideal condition
from the schoolmaster's point of view would be one
in which boys entered school at a fixed age, having
passed through a regular preparatory training of
a uniform character suitable to their age and ability.
This would be the case where boys proceeded from
preparatory schools affiliated to the school for older
boys. In the schools preparatory to the great public
boarding schools the character of the education given
is comparatively uniform, and the boys in passing
from the one to the other continue their studies
progressively. There is no complete break or
change of system. This is possibly the case also
with many of the London day schools. But in the
north of England at any rate things are very
different. The entry of new boys at the beginning
of each term is of a most heterogeneous character.
The private schools which serve as preparatory
schools have as a general rule no sort of connexion
with the grammar schools, and the character of the
education which they give varies very widely. Some
are good, with others it is difficult at times to ascer-
tain what the subjects of instruction can have been.
Besides the boys from private, there are boys from
the elementary schools. In a first grade school
in the south of England probably few boys have
received their early training in an elementary school.
In the north of England it is by no means uncommon,
not simply in the case of boys who are receiving

a free education upon the foundation, but in the case of boys who are paying the school fees. One of the assistant Commissioners to the Royal Commission of 1894 noted with surprise the number of 'white turned-down collars, the recognized mark of a comfortable, well-to-do home, in a board school of a Lancashire town.' The feeling would not be the same in all towns, and the practice in a rough colliery town would differ from the practice in a manufacturing town. Where a boy comes from the primary school at the age of eleven or twelve, having passed the fifth or sixth standard, there is little difficulty in fitting him into a first grade school. At the best he will be a 'competent reader and speller and expert in Arithmetic,' and have begun Algebra. His English Grammar, however, consists mainly in the power of drawing elaborate tables of sentence analysis, too cumbrous for youthful understanding. He has little or no knowledge of English History, and has only occasionally learnt any foreign language. The boy who comes from the private preparatory school will be worse at Arithmetic and Writing as a rule, but at the best his English work will be superior; he will have more knowledge and power of expression, and will have made a start with either French or Latin. Under the schemes of the Charity Commission many endowed schools are required to reserve scholarships for boys coming from the elementary schools. This arrangement works well when the elementary schools make an effort to prepare their boys for taking these scholarships. In the district of which I am chiefly speaking the local School Boards are taking some pains to teach the elements of Latin to their boys, and this is a step in the right direction. The world of education, like other worlds, is ruled by phrases. At present it is common to hear it urged that the true scientific method is to proceed from 'the known to the unknown.' This is interpreted to mean that English and English Grammar are 'the known' and come first. I prefer to believe still that 'a great deal of Grammar which it is very hard to explain to a learner becomes clear without any explanation at all in the mere act of learning a foreign language[1].' It must be an immense advantage to Welsh elementary education as compared with English that boys and girls are compelled to be bilingual.

It is when we have to deal with older boys that the connexion between elementary and secondary schools becomes a matter of difficulty. How is a boy of fourteen, or it may be fifteen, who has learned nothing of any foreign language, to be placed in a secondary school, even if in some directions he gives evidence of knowledge and ability? Such boys have passed through the standards, and gone from the lower elementary into the Higher Grade Schools or Schools of Science. I have no wish to undervalue the work which has been done by these schools. It is recognized that

[1] *Report of Schools Inquiry Commission*, 1868, p. 23.

they have supplied a want in English education, and have been the means of giving instruction to numbers of children for a longer time than they would otherwise have received it. But as far as first grade day schools are concerned, these schools have not served as a link between elementary and higher education. The best pupils from the elementary schools who now proceed as foundation scholars to the grammar schools do not come from the higher grade schools. They come through the personal interest of some school manager, clergyman or minister, and not through the working of machinery inaugurated by a board or committee. The regulations of the Science and Art Department, the fairy godmother of the higher grade system, have now, it is true, been so far relaxed as to make it possible to give some literary training in the Schools of Science, and it should be possible in the future to make the transference of boys more easy from higher grade to grammar schools. It must not be forgotten that an increasing number of grammar schools are forming themselves into 'Schools of Science' under the Science and Art Department, and are therefore giving an education similar in character to that of the higher grade Board schools. The time, however, which has to be allotted to Science and Art subjects is still excessive for schools of the grammar-school type. It not unfrequently happens that a boy whose education has been mainly in the

Science and Art subjects comes to a grammar school with the intention of learning foreign languages, and would be heartbroken at the idea of being placed in the lowest form of a classical or modern side, to which his linguistic attainments would naturally doom him, in spite of a sheaf of South Kensington certificates.   In a large grammar school there are opportunities of overcoming most difficulties of classification in one way or another, as sufficiently large groups of boys of similar age and attainments can generally be formed.   In a small school the difficulties must be almost insurmountable, and are in no way diminished by the fact that these older boys from the elementary schools often only intend to come to the local grammar school for a short time, in order to finish their education at the socially more important school, and thereby improve their chance of getting a good situation in business.   Such boys when they leave are no fair test of the value of a grammar-school education, and can only make English schoolmasters look with envy upon the regular gradations of the nine- and six-year courses of the *Gymnasien* and *Realschulen* of Germany.   There is no external pressure, like that of the conscription, in England to make parents appreciate the value of a sound education.   But apart from such violent compulsion, the remedies lie in a closer affiliation of private and preparatory to public schools, a better understanding between elementary and secondary schools by which the passage from the one to the other can be rendered more easy and profitable, and a clearer acquaintance on the part of parents with the distinctions between the different kinds of schools and the education which they give.

Having now considered the character of the material which enters a day school, we may pass on to questions of internal organization. The difficulties which confront the schoolmaster in dealing with the classical side of a school are time-honoured and familiar. Upon a classical side there are boys who are intending to proceed to the older Universities, there are those whose school education ends with the matriculation examination of London or Victoria University and other examinations which serve as entrance to the professions, and there are those whose parents regard the general education of a classical side as the best preparation for after-life. What are the subjects which must form part of a liberal education? what amount of time is to be assigned to them? when is the proper period for specialization in study, and to what lengths shall it be carried? These and other similar questions have to be answered, but they are questions which are in no sense peculiar to day schools, and therefore I may be allowed to pass them over.

It is rather when we turn to the modern and science sides of a day school that peculiar difficulties of organization begin. Boys who join the classical side of a school, whether intended for the University or not, nearly all remain a sufficient time to complete their education; their parents have received a similar training themselves, have been through the regular mill and wish their sons to go through it, or else are ambitious for them to win University distinction and join the professional classes. There is a reigning tradition, and, except when the Greek or Latin Verse collar chafes, but little rebellion against it. But on a modern side there is no reign of tradition. Educational authorities cannot yet be said to have established one, neither has the general public. I have already spoken of the different ages of the boys at entrance—varying from ten to fifteen—all having learnt Arithmetic and English, and a few, though the number is increasing, having learnt a little French, or in rare cases Latin; some intending to receive their education wholly at the grammar school, others intending to stay only for a short time, that in the search for a situation they may gain the advantage of calling themselves grammar-school boys. The average time spent at school by boys upon the modern side of a day school is much shorter than the average of a classical side. It would be very rare indeed for a boy to stay the six years of the course of a German *Realschule*. This is the real problem of modern-side education. If it were the rule for boys to come to school for a specified and sufficient time, there would be no great difficulty in finding a satisfactory course of study. At present

the variety of standard and aim is too great. There
is a highest form perhaps in which the boys are
able to take the Oxford and Cambridge Higher
Certificate examination; there are middle forms in
which boys remain till the age of sixteen; and then
again there are lower forms in which boys leave
school at a still earlier age, having only reached
a rudimentary standard of attainment. The difficulty
is to provide a scheme of education sufficiently
graded to suit them all. As the boys are intended
for business pursuits, it is necessary to consider what
form of education is best adapted for the purpose.
But commercial education is a phrase which as yet
has little definite meaning. Some points are of
course agreed upon. Good writing and arithmetic
are essential. Then there is drawing, the importance
of which is now generally recognized. As to short-
hand and book-keeping, commercial arithmetic, and
other such subjects, they are not regular parts of
a liberal education. Their proper place comes in
extra classes, for which opportunity should be provided. The same applies to manual instruction,
except in the case of quite young boys, when it can
be made a valuable part of the regular work.

There is an interesting letter from a practical
business man published in the Assistant Com-
missioner's Report on the County of Devon to the
late Royal Commission on Secondary Education,
which represents very well the general notion of the
requirements of ordinary business life. From this it

will be seen that the boy should write a good hand, have learnt drawing, and be able to compose a business letter from general instructions. Book-keeping is reckoned among the elementary subjects, but here it may be urged that as different firms have different systems of book-keeping, it is better for the boy to have a mastery of arithmetic which will enable him to learn any required system. Beyond these subjects, foreign languages, art instruction, or practical science, are suggested according to the particular branch of commerce or industry the boy is intended to pursue. Over and above the regular requirements it is urged that a course of applied logic, for the training of the reasoning faculty, and a knowledge of the rudiments of political economy, are necessary. In the ordinary grammar-school education the training of the reasoning faculty is given through the medium of the teaching of language and grammatical analysis and the different branches of mathematics. The elements of political economy are only taught to a few older boys, and neither this subject nor logic could readily be made a profitable means of instruction for younger boys. The art of ready reasoning and common sense must always remain in great part gifts of nature.

Apart from the subjects already named there are the usual school studies of history, geography, and English literature. History and geography have their commercial side, but the object of school teaching must rather be to provide the foundation upon which the studies of commercial history and geography can afterwards be based. The more special study of such matters, as well as of commercial law or political economy, is more appropriate to places of advanced instruction, such as University Colleges and places of technical education. Secondary schools must fix their chief attention upon more general aims. The teaching of English literature is a matter of difficulty upon a modern side. The commercial side of this subject, if we may so speak, is the art of writing a good business letter, which for school purposes we must include under the general head of the art of composition. But apart from such questions and as a matter of liberal education the teaching of English literature has its difficulty. The boys have received no training in Latin, and consequently have a very limited knowledge of their own language. Many of our classical writers are only half intelligible unless there is some previous knowledge of Latin, and it is only in the higher forms of a modern side that the easiest essay of Macaulay can be read, because of the number of Latin derivatives which all need explanation.

English children, it seems to be admitted, do not receive the same careful instruction in their own language as French and German children do in their native tongues. Before the Commission of 1868 Professor Seeley urged that boys should be trained in the gift of speech, 'taught to use it more freely, more skilfully, more precisely, and to admire and to

enjoy it more when it is nobly used by great authors.'
Brilliancy and elegance should be put before precision and accuracy.   It remains now however, as
then, a fact that average teachers are average men
with little brilliancy or elegance in their nature, and
'that for one man who can take a play of Shakspear
or the *Paradise Lost* as a class book, there are ten
who can carry boys very respectably through Caesar
and Virgil, whether regard be had to the language or
the subject-matter[1].'

Without neglecting English literature, precision
and accuracy must be sought through other means.
The main part of grammar-school education is, as it
always has been, the study of language, 'the liberal
science or art of grammar, the ground and fountain
of all the other liberal arts and sciences which surge
and spring out of the same,' as an old founder
expresses it.   This is the chief instrument of instruction and means of mental discipline.   On a modern
side this training must be derived from the modern
languages, and then a question arises as to which
language or languages shall be chosen.   It may
seem obvious to reply French and German, but if
the end in view is commercial utility the answer is
not always clear.   I have, for instance, been told by
parents that Italian and Spanish are commercially
the most important foreign languages.   On the other
hand, I have been told with equal confidence that
German is the one language needful.   All depends

---

[1] *Report of Schools Inquiry Commission*, 1868, pp. 25, 26.

upon the trade in which the speakers are engaged. Again, it is only in a few towns that any foreign language is of real practical importance. In some towns of Lancashire French and German would be considered of no greater utility than Latin and Greek. From an educational point of view there is no doubt that for boys who know no Latin, German is the best language as a first step. It is more akin to English, its sounds are comparatively easy for English tongues, and it has a more obvious accidence. French is an unsatisfactory language for an English boy to begin with. A clever boy can make progress, but the average boy seems to find French too impalpable; the distinctions of sound are too fine, the grammatical idioms too subtle. Better progress is made afterwards with French if a boy begins his study of foreign languages through German. As to the amount of progress that can be made, it is all a question of time. If the boys stop long enough, English day schools can produce perfectly good results in the teaching of foreign languages; and there are now a sufficient number of Englishmen well qualified to act as teachers. The great obstacle is the fact that the majority of boys do not stop long enough at school to obtain any real mastery of a language. There are no generally accepted tests of a modern-side education either for parents or employers. There is no leaving certificate, as in Germany, which is required by all good firms of their clerks: there is no compulsory military service of which such a certificate will lessen the length. Boys leave school when their parents think that it is time for them to be getting to work, and not because they have reached any definite stage in their education. If leaders of commerce required boys to give evidence of a certain standard of attainment before they would give them employment, then those standards would be reached. But the bulk of parents and commercial men regard fifteen or sixteen as the proper age for leaving school. At that age boys are not above the necessity of passing through the humdrum duties of office and other routine. This being the general feeling, boys themselves are anxious to get to work early and to exchange the restraint of school for what they regard as the greater freedom of business life. From the school-master's side, whether regarded as a mental discipline and cultivation or for purposes of proficiency in the subjects taught, modern-side education would be more satisfactory if it lasted longer. If complaint is made of English modern-side education as compared with continental schools, English schoolmasters may fairly reply that if they were given similar conditions they could do just as well.

Of natural science teaching I have already spoken in dealing with the Science and Art Department. It would almost seem as if the advocates of natural science were at present suffering from the effects of too great a success. There is no doubt that science so called is often taught too early and too exclusively,

before the reasoning faculty has been properly developed by other studies; and experience shows that
boys who begin in this way are easily caught up
by boys who begin the study of natural science at
a later age. It is no uncommon thing in secondary
schools to hear a wish expressed by science masters
that the boys who come to them should have received
no previous science teaching. It is also not an
unknown thing to find University professors uttering
the same wish with reference to boys coming up to the
University. The temptation to science teaching is
that almost all boys can make something of science,
at any rate in the earlier stages; but, if begun too
early and too exclusively, it is not the best instrument
of mental training.

In a large school there will always be boys with
an aptitude for science, who intend to go to the
University for purposes of medical or other scientific
study. There are also boys intended for engineering,
chemical industries, and the like, who wish to give
more attention to scientific subjects during the last
part of their time at school. Fifteen appears to be
the earliest age at which this can profitably be done.
Many complaints have been made of premature
specialization, and the charge is more particularly
pressed against the teaching of natural science and
mathematics in schools. It is a necessity that boys
who wish to obtain a scholarship in mathematics or
natural science, that is to say the assistance necessary
in order to enable them to proceed to the University,

should give the chief part of their last years at school to these subjects. The reason is that the Colleges require not merely evidence of ability, but an amount of actual knowledge which can only be obtained by specialization. At the younger Universities, such as Victoria, the entrance examinations require evidence of a good general education; at the older Universities, such an examination as Responsions at Oxford represents the required level. To boys who have been on the classical side before they devote their time more especially to mathematics or science, such an examination as Responsions presents few terrors. It is different in the case of a modern-side boy who at a late age decides to go to the University and who has up till that time learnt no Latin or Greek. It is hard for him to have to acquire the requisite amount of classics at the same time that he is obliged to devote more of his time to his own special study of natural science. It can scarcely, however, be contended that a minimum of the classics is undesirable, considering the extent to which scientific nomenclature lays the Latin and Greek languages under contribution. These however are questions which are common to all schools, and I must not dwell upon them further. Throughout I have confined myself to the practical difficulties of school organization. It must not be supposed that such a mode of treatment exhausts all the possibilities of life in a day school.

J. E. KING.

THE TUTORIAL SYSTEM

I⊤ is often the fate of an institution to be known to the mass of mankind by one or more of its separable accidents, and consequently to be judged by them, and esteemed or despised, without much reference to its essential qualities. Now the Tutorial System has long been connected, in most men's minds, with an elaborate double-barrelled arrangement for the correction of Latin verses, set by one man and looked over by another; a labour which is believed to consume the greater part of the tutor's time and to produce very inadequate results in the education of the boys. It must be partly in consequence of this association that we find the newer public schools, in framing their constitutions, disregarding the Tutorial System altogether, though many of them were formed, in other respects, mainly on the lines of Rugby. Men who have lived under the system, learnt under it, taught under it, become perhaps head-masters of other schools where it does not exist, and thenceforward hardly allude, in their writings and speeches on educational subjects, to what seems, to those left behind, a part of the order of nature. Is the Tutorial System, then, an out-of-date, cumbersome survival, passing away into limbo with the exclusively classical curriculum, perhaps with Latin verses themselves? Or has it a future, and can merits be claimed for it which render it worthy of the consideration of reformers and legislators who are devising ideal methods of education?

In view of the general drift of modern opinion, the practical question is whether the framework of such a system is, or is not, capable of being adapted to suit a wider and more comprehensive scheme of liberal education than was contained in the 'grand old fortifying classical curriculum.' Cannot the principle, if it be right in theory, of attaching each boy, more or less closely, to one man during the whole of his school career, be judged on its own merits, apart from excrescences which loom so large in the eyes of outside observers? It must in fairness be admitted that some of the more uncompromising advocates of the old style of education, those who have fought inch by inch against the claims of modern subjects, have been inclined to lend colour to the same view, namely that the Tutorial System is inextricably bound up with the said excrescences. We at Eton have heard it said, ' The weekly theme has already been abolished; and if a tutor is not to correct his pupil's verses, what is there left to justify his existence?' So the younger men, after an occasional protest and a frequent grumble, have one by one acquiesced, influenced by a vague fear that the wheat may be rooted up with what they strongly suspect to be tares; advancing years have improved the necessary knack, and each man reads through about a thousand verses a week, correcting and perhaps re-writing half of them.

It is therefore not unnatural that to the world at large the system should be known by its weakest, or at any rate its most questionable points, as an ingenious method for wasting the largest possible amount of time with the smallest possible results. The tutor's main function, it is said, consists in writing verses for the admiration, or amusement, of the division-master; while by way of revenge, to take the wind out of the sails of the division-master, the lessons are construed over to the tutor by his pupils before they say them in school, as though to secure the maximum of dullness for the twice-told tale.

This is not the place to defend or to attack the exaltation of Latin verse or the 'construing' system, nor to explain the judicious modifications introduced of late years into this part of the work. Even granting all that can be urged by the most advanced critic of such methods and subjects of education, we may fairly ask whether there are not elements in the Tutorial System which should entitle it to a place in future arrangements, and which may possibly help to solve some of the vexed questions which are pressing upon us.

But before advancing suggestions which must be merely tentative, and which are likely to appear highly disputable, it may be best to lay down three propositions to which no general opposition need be expected.

1. The principle of entrusting to one man the education of a boy from the age of thirteen to that of nineteen is a natural and obvious one.

2. The Tutorial System has been valued, adopted, and extended by some of those whose names stand highest among practical educators.

3. In practice and in fact there are advantages gained under the Tutorial System, both by masters and boys, which are quite independent of the particular form in which it is established in any given school.

1. This statement requires a little development to prevent it from being a somewhat otiose truism. When parents divest themselves of a portion of their parental responsibility, by entrusting to others the direction of their child's education, the natural step is to appoint some one person to supervise that education, to be a permanently responsible guide and controller. Even so, it is obvious that there may be every gradation of nearness or remoteness in the relation of the person so appointed to the child: at one end of the scale the Mentor or Chiron, the

Bossuet or Fénélon, who is able to devote himself entirely to the study of the child's intellect and character, and the bestowal of the mental food most suited to the due development thereof; at the other the παιδαγωγός, whose duty it is to take or send the child to skilled instructors provided by school or university. The practical question for public schools is at what point between these two extremes they shall draw the line : how far it is possible and advisable, without undue overlapping or waste of time, for the boy to be in a real, and not nominal, relation to one man during the whole of his school life; and whether that one man should, or should not, be the director of his studies.

Now in the earlier days of public schools, till perhaps rather more than a century ago, there was not much room for doubt on this point; the parent confided the boy to the head-master, to be educated by him. The exact date at which this view, still rightly held in theory, became in practice unworkable, varied in different schools, as their growth in size rendered it gradually more and more obvious that of the younger boys none but prize-winners or rascals could hope for close personal contact with the head-master. Speaking broadly, we **may** say that the natural result followed both in day schools and in boarding schools. In day schools the principle of permanence was sacrificed, the education and charge of the boy being committed to the form-master for the time being ; though it is interesting to note in this

connexion that at University College School the
multiplication of studies and consequent dislocation
of the time-table have dethroned the form-master in
his turn, as it was felt that his knowledge of the
individual boys might be reduced to somewhat
shadowy dimensions : this has led to the institution
of 'consulting-masters,' each boy being assigned to
one permanently during his school career.   Thus we
see the germ of a Tutorial System springing up in
a somewhat unexpected quarter.

In boarding schools, on the other hand, the obvious
and logical principle would seem to be, to hand over
the control of the boy's education, as well as the
general charge of him, to the house-master, or, where
the system of separate houses is not adopted, to
a tutor specially appointed to have control over some
unit, a dormitory or the like.   This arrangement has
been adopted in the main in most schools, perhaps in
all that have been founded this century ; but it has
the obvious defect, from the educational point of
view, that while the curriculum remained chiefly
classical, non-classical house-masters were appointed,
who could not be expected to control and guide the
main part of a boy's studies.   Consequently, in these
schools, the permanent director of a boy has had but
little to do with his education.   On the other hand,
the question was complicated, both at Eton and at
Rugby, and to a certain extent also at Harrow,
by the fact that boys did not, as a rule, lodge with
the masters at all, but at boarding houses under the

charge of dames or others who had nothing to do with the work of education. Hence we find—first, wealthy or ambitious parents paying young University graduates to come and live in the place, and supplement their boys' education ; next, masters in the school receiving a fee to act as private tutors ; thirdly, a rule established that every boy was to have a tutor. This may be an inexact account of a somewhat obscure period of scholastic history ; but at any rate at Eton we find, at the time of the Public Schools Commission in 1864, a distinction still existing between being 'tutor' to a boy and being 'private tutor,' the master in the former case receiving only half the fee, but doing exactly the same work as he did in the latter. In the meantime masters were taking over the boarding houses : Dr. Arnold decreed at Rugby that none but masters were to succeed to them, and the same rule was enforced at Eton a few years later. But the principle was before this thoroughly established that every boy should have a tutor, who was to be responsible for his work and conduct throughout his school life, and to be directly engaged in educating him. If the house-master was a classical man, the boys in his house were naturally members of his pupil-room ; if not, there was to a certain extent a dual control, the complications of which have been gradually solving themselves of late years. How far it is essential or advisable that a master should be tutor to the boys in his house, is a question that will be discussed later. It does not directly affect the present point, which may be re-stated as follows : it seems, *a priori*, natural and desirable that each boy in a large school should be intimately attached to some one master, who can watch and help the development of his intellect and character.

2. It may be permissible to quote a few high authorities who have spoken with strong approval of the Tutorial System, and who, with full power to alter or modify, have favoured or increased its domain. It will be advisable to exclude present head-masters, and also those who, having been tutors themselves, might be suspected of a tendency to magnify their office. For instance, in giving evidence before the Public Schools Commission, man after man described the system, under various figures, but all to the same purport, as the 'pivot,' the 'keystone,' the 'backbone,' the 'cornerstone' of the arrangements of the school to which he belonged. Passing from these to more unbiassed observers, we find Dr. Arnold exalting and amplifying the powers of the tutors at Rugby, introducing in addition something like the 'private business' of Eton, and speaking in high terms of the value of the institution in drawing closer the relations between master and boys and in stimulating the men to keenness and self-cultivation. It must be remembered that he was himself educated at Winchester, where the system did not exist; and that he, if any one, approached scholastic questions with an open mind, and with that oft-quoted tendency to 'wake every morning

with the impression that everything is an open question.'

The present Archbishop of Canterbury, in his evidence before the Public Schools Commission as head-master of Rugby, spoke of the system as beneficial both intellectually and morally, and 'would certainly introduce it into any new school of which he had the organization, unless it were a very small school.' His definition of the system is broadly and clearly expressed in the following words: 'It is a good thing in a large school, taking the work which is done by the boy, to divide it into two parts, one of which shall be done with each form-master successively, and the other of which shall be done with some one master who is to have charge of him from the beginning of his time to the end.'

The present Master of Trinity, as head-master of Harrow, before the same Commission, spoke strongly of the value of the intimate relation between tutor and pupil, both for the intellectual progress and for the moral well-being of the boys. He laid particular stress on the advantage of the combination of the two: 'The truth is that by far the most accurate means that a man has of judging of the moral condition of a boy, except in very exceptional cases, is by observing his intellectual progress.' Such testimony, from men of high enlightenment, endowed as they were with the power and the will to change what they found defective, goes far to prove that there are elements in the system which ought not to be lightly sacrificed to any craving for symmetry or convenience, or to the crowding claims of a super-fluity of subjects. We may not go all the way with those other witnesses who evidently held, and almost said, that 'it is conceivable that human wisdom might have devised something more perfect' (than the Tutorial System), 'but it is certain that it never did'; but we, who have been brought up under it, and know something of what it has been in the past, can hardly fail to have a strong wish to

> Keep the young generations in hail,
> And bequeath them no tumbled house.

For that there is a tendency to undermine it at the present day is tolerably obvious.

3. Certain advantages, both to masters and boys, seem to flow more naturally from the Tutorial System than from any other. Such a saying as Dr. Arnold's, 'No parochial ministry can be more properly a cure of souls than yours,' though appropriate enough to any schoolmaster, must come home still more closely to the tutor. The feeling, 'if my pupil leaves school uneducated or unprincipled, mine is the fault,' may sometimes make our punishment greater than we can bear, but it can hardly fail to have a sobering and elevating effect on our work and conduct. As to the intimacy and friendship, we may sometimes be tempted to exaggerate this, and it is salutary to turn to the evidence before the same Commission, and to note how some tutors draw rose-coloured and Utopian pictures, culminating in the artless statement of one

man, 'a boy loves his tutor, as a general rule, very much'; then to find, a few pages later, the bluff words of a boy, 'No, I do not think the tutor is *in loco parentis* to a boy: I do not think we looked upon him as doing anything more than just teaching us.' But between these two extremes there is room for many gradations of intimacy and attachment: and it is claimed that under the Tutorial System they have a much better chance of arising in the case of the average man and the average boy, while without it any close ties would seem likely to be confined to prominent boys or to exceptional men.

It is to the young master and the young boy that the advantages are perhaps most obvious. A young boy, fresh from a private school, is at first apt to be simply lost in a form and in the house of which he is so insignificant a unit. Very salutary for him, no doubt; but there is a gain, the reality of which has been proved over and over again, in putting him also in a more homely and human relation with some one. From the hours spent in the semi-official atmosphere of pupil-room, with all their drudgery and dullness, their occasional storms, their occasional gleams of sunshine, there can, and does, bloom the fine flower of confidence and mutual understanding: troubles and difficulties are related, advice is asked, the boy feels quite early in his school life that he has a friend upon whom to lean. Let not those be offended who are conscious of achieving splendid results in this direction under other systems. All that is claimed is that under this system it is more natural, more easy, more obvious.

Then again, there is no one element in a public school so important as the young masters. One who is himself no longer a young master may be forgiven for asserting this somewhat dogmatically. But indeed there is no necessity to insist upon the point, for there seems at this moment to be a general consensus thereon. Theorists and practical men are uniting to claim that previous training must be bestowed upon the beginner, so that he may enter upon his duties full-fledged, instead of having to learn and unlearn much for himself. Again, it is being strongly urged in some quarters that it is a wasteful mistake to put young men in their fresh vigour to teach the lowest forms, and that the highest and most interesting work should be assigned to them. Also 'Retirement Schemes' are warning us that grey hairs will soon be no more seen in class-rooms. The tendency to appoint athletes may be taken as pointing in the same direction; for the qualities thereby secured are not likely to endure, at any rate in their first intention, for more than the first ten years of a man's career as a master. Now, the Tutorial System is obviously contrived to make the most of the younger men, and to give them responsibility and varied experience from the first, with opportunities bounded only by their willingness and ability to make use of them. Practice in dealing with boys of all ages on an intimate footing is also of vast advantage to them when they come to be house-masters. The unfairness of confining these advantages to classical men leads us to a different branch of the subject, and may be used as a convenient peg on which to hang a few disconnected thoughts, hardly to be dignified with the name of opinions or suggestions, as to the possibility of adapting the Tutorial System to schools which are not mainly classical.

The system, adopted at Clifton and elsewhere, of attaching a young man to each house, with the title of house-tutor, as a kind of 'understudy' to the house-master, seems in many respects quite admirable. To describe and discuss it would take too much space, even if it were not presumptuous in one who has had no personal experience of it. But it evidently differs from the Tutorial System proper in three points; first, that the relation between the house-tutor and the boys is not necessarily an educational one; secondly, that there is not the same independence and 'free hand,' with the corresponding fullness of responsibility that ought to be so stimulating and inspiring to a young man; thirdly, that the benefits are only open to a limited number, and that those excluded from the privileged circle will probably be the youngest men, to whom the added interest and scope for developing themselves would be valuable. But is it not possible to some extent to combine the benefits of this arrangement with those of the older Tutorial System, and thereby to do

something towards easing the growing difficulties
caused by the multiplication of subjects taught in
school, complicated as they are by the wish to allow
boys to 'specialize' in the subjects wherein they
show promise? And may not some such scheme
have a value for day-schools also, by adopting and
extending the principle of ' consulting-masters '
alluded to above, giving them the title and functions of tutor, with not only the supervision, but the
management of a boy's education? There is a mistaken idea that the system is only applicable in a
limited number of schools, those attended by sons
of wealthy parents, who can afford the luxury of
a private tutor. Surely, if it be in itself desirable,
it can be adapted to any school. A parent pays,
under the head of tuition, a certain sum, large or
small: a proportion of this can be assigned by the
authorities as a tutor's fee. Another objection, *in
pari materia*, was started by the Public Schools
Commissioners. It was several times asked whether
a man might not be tempted, owing to the fact that
he derived far the greater part of his income from
the tutorial work, to neglect his work in school, and
devote all his powers to his pupils. While the possibility was allowed, it was asserted confidently that
the facts were otherwise; and in the generation
that has since elapsed, with the amount of form-work
increased and better organized, the opposite danger
is a far more real one. The time which a man has
to spare from his more public duties has gradually

diminished : the average boy spends quite enough hours over his books, if he does his school work conscientiously : and consequently, in two directions, we find a considerable difference between ourselves and the tutors of a generation ago. These are : (1) the boy's general education, (2) the securing of his rapid advance in his 'strong' subject, if he has one. For the former we are apt to trust vaguely to the multiplication of school subjects ; for the latter we send him to a specialist, with an extra fee, or if he be a classical scholar we trust mainly to the excellent division-teaching in the upper part of the school. It was noticeable that in a recent discussion upon the growing diminution in the number of Eton boys who obtain the highest classical honours at Cambridge, the various remedies proposed hardly touched upon the tutor's share of the work. Yet, in the days of our fathers, if a boy obtained high honours at the University, it was recognized as in great measure due to his tutor. And again, on the other point, a boy of no great powers at classics often found and developed some special bent, owing to his tutor's insight and guidance. A keen antiquarian was heard to say the other day, ' I never was any good at Greek and Latin, but my tutor used to take me by myself at Private, and read the Anglo-Saxon Chronicle with me.' Is it not then conceivable that something might be gained by deliberately putting more time, and more subjects, at the disposal of the tutor, whose distinct duties should be broadly twofold: (1) to see that each boy makes real and rapid progress, according to his powers, in the line for which he has a taste, or which his future career renders desirable; (2) to see to the general education, especially in English, of each boy. Thus a boy intended for the army, or the diplomatic service, or a commercial career, would probably be assigned from the outset to a modern language, mathematical, or scientific tutor.

There are two objections certain to be made, as to each of which a few words may be said. First, that the best and most effective teaching in a school is admittedly the class teaching, and that any diminution of this would be a retrograde movement, a sort of attempt to put new wine into old bottles, and to bolster up a system that has had its day. But, allowing every merit to class-teaching, and assuming it to be of the very best quality, is there not a constant effort required to keep all but the very best boys from frequently relapsing into one or other of two warped views of their teacher's relation to them: (1) that he is the task-master, to be appeased or circumvented; (2) that he is the pourer out of streams of information, and they the empty buckets sitting to be filled, praiseworthy if they prove not Danaids' buckets? In other words, does it come naturally or easily within his province to teach boys how to learn? Does not this require a closer and more individual relation and a longer acquaintance?

The second objection will be that if you assign

a boy at once to a tutor in what is to be his special subject, you are anticipating, and even aggravating, the evils of specialization which are now so generally recognized. This may be met on two sides. First, the curtailing of the school work will enable a carefully chosen curriculum, varying in different schools, to be imposed without hardship on all boys alike. Secondly, the more of a specialist a man is, the more alive is he likely to be to the dangers of early specialization, and the more thankful for the chance of extending his own interests, concurrently with the boys'; with the knowledge that his, and his alone, will be the fault if the pupil turns out lamentably ignorant in any branch of a liberal education, after he has been his tutor, with plenty of time at his disposal, for five or six years. Besides, it has generally been assumed, on somewhat insufficient grounds, that a classical master is competent to teach history, modern as well as ancient, geography, divinity, and something of English, not to mention a modern language or two, and perhaps the elementary mathematics. Is it too much to assume that the non-classical man may possibly show himself, when he gets the chance, equally many-sided? We shall all be very shallow, it may be said, and it is better to do one thing well than ten indifferently. But we may remember that it was Dr. Arnold's wish that every master should teach every subject; and it is as true now as when Professor Seeley said it a generation ago, that a school is not a university, and that profound learning in the teachers is not requisite to the same extent at the former as it is at the latter.

With a larger proportion of the work set free from the stimulus of marks and examinations, will there not be a gain in a direction where many thoughtful observers have noticed a growing evil? A boy, especially a quick and promising boy, is more and more inclined to take a view of his work which may be described as that of 'small profits and quick returns.' Full marks for his next exercise, distinction in his next examination—these are the legitimate aims upon which duty and self-interest alike direct his gaze. Does not the same tendency account for the growing difficulty we experience in inducing the more able boys to accept advice as to private reading, especially of English? Few of them have an operative belief that no performance of tasks, however perfect, under any curriculum, however well chosen, will suffice of itself to make them educated men. Will not every tutor have a far better chance of raising the heads of the good and docile sheep from cropping the pastures at their feet all the time, and pointing them to the higher slopes of the mountain?

There remain two points to be very briefly considered: the number of pupils to whom one man can do justice, and the relation of the tutor to the housemaster

The powers of men vary, and some of our predecessors must have been able to dispense with sleep, as it is notorious that they dispensed with exercise. Men still living speak of having had ninety pupils, and seem to imply that they did for them all that was requisite or desirable. We find a Harrow master admitting to the Public Schools Commission that he was tutor to sixty-three boys, adding, 'It is a very large family, certainly.' The questioner, with some surprise, 'Sixty-three boys, to all of whom you are *in loco parentis*?' The answer is instructive: 'Just so; but a great number require little extraordinary care.' Did he perhaps mean 'extraordinarily little care'? It may be that we are feebler folk than they were; but if you call yourself a boy's tutor, one hour a week would not seem an excessive amount of your thought and attention for him to claim individually. A simple sum shows that sixty-three pupils would thus take up nine hours a day, including Sundays. Perhaps from twenty to thirty would seem a reasonable limit, giving, as it would do, a chance for every master to have a fair number of pupils.

Opinions will undoubtedly differ as to the relation, where the house-master is not also tutor, between the two authorities. Some such arrangement as the Clifton one, alluded to before, would seem natural, a master of modern subjects being attached to each classical master's house, and *vice versa*. That the tutor, having the control of a boy's time and constant association with him, should also be responsible for his religious education, should prepare him for Confirmation, should correspond with his parents, would seem natural to some : while others would like these important duties reserved for the older and more experienced man.   Be this as it may, any conflict or jealousy should surely be impossible between two men whose sole objects are the good of the boys and the good of the school.

Even if the variety of subjects make it necessary for the boys in any one house to be subdivided among three or four different tutors, and confusion and inconvenience be anticipated therefrom, we may point to the case of the Collegers at Eton, who, at any given time, are divided among some eighteen or twenty different pupil-rooms, without preventing College from being as united a body as could well be found in a public school.   For them, at any rate, the principle of a permanent relation to one man, based upon responsibility for their education, has been found to work well and produce good results.   If applied to less able scholars with the addition of 'free-trade,' or a wider choice of subjects wherein the tutor may give special aid and attention, it is possible that the Tutorial System may bear fruit in the future on a more extensive scale.

C. LOWRY.

SOME PROBLEMS CONNECTED WITH
THE TEACHING OF SIXTH FORMS

A sign of the times is to be seen in the position
and importance assigned nowadays to the Sixth
Form Tutor.   Called in early days by a less
dignified title, his duties were few, his hours of work
nominal, and his excuse for existence was the need
for relieving the head-master of composition teaching
and for having some one ready to carry on work
with the Sixth Form in the head-master's absence.
In many schools at the present moment the old
'compos cad' would scarcely know himself.   He is
responsible not only for the composition work, but
for a large bulk of the regular reading of the form ;
to him are entrusted, for what is practically special
tuition, those Sixth Form boys who will be candidates
for University scholarships ; and not only will he
be expected to teach them to hunt for scholarships
successfully, but his advice will often be asked by
parents and head-master as to the destiny of the
boys under his care.   It is again important in our
large public boarding schools, where the Prefect

system is the key to the position, that the Sixth
Form tutor should be in sympathy and close touch
with at least the main body of the prefects; and in
the thousand details of public school life in which
he will be invited to interest himself, he will often
be assigned the place of honour and looked to as an
authority. His opportunities are infinite, and his
field of work inexhaustible.

Leaving this ground, and the discussion to which
it leads, we may well inquire into the meaning
of the change which has been made in the function of a Sixth Form teacher, and, with it, in the
treatment of a Sixth Form.

First of all it means that the Sixth Form see
much less, in some schools practically nothing,
of their head-master as a teacher. Indeed it is
commonly said that the chief quality expected in a
head-master is power of 'organization,' a somewhat
vague term, which probably means the capacity for
managing his staff. Learning, a student's tastes
and habits, even inspiration as a teacher, are often
regarded as quite subsidiary qualifications, or else as
luxuries and even dangerous. No doubt the head-
master has many other means and opportunities of
making an impression upon boys, and particularly
upon his leaders and prefects, but it is—at any rate
to my mind—a very open question whether it is
possible for him to understand the temperament,
character, capacities, or sympathies of any boy without the intellectual give and take of every-day life

in the class-room. And I suppose that nine-tenths of the things said and done by a head-master, which left the permanent impression, gave a new meaning to things, and quickened the best interests, were said and done on the spur of the moment in the Sixth Form room, and suggested by some accident in the course of the lesson. No head-master, I imagine, nowadays, if Sixth Form boys are to be found in other departments than the Classical Sixth, would neglect the opportunity of combining them in one body for at least a few lessons a week, and none would consider this the least important occasion for creating close relations with the head boys of his school. Then why, it may be asked, is it in these days more necessary for a head-master to organize than to teach? Why does he, not willingly perhaps, but of necessity, resign to a deputy those very duties which Arnold considered his golden opportunities and the things which made his life worth living?

There are other spheres of activity in which we seem to have gone a little crazy with the cry to organize. At bottom there is perhaps one reason to account for it everywhere; in schools at any rate it is in a large measure due to the widening of the field of education, the attempt to provide for all sorts of careers, the appeal made by the Government and the public to the head-masters to send them candidates for public examinations straight from the schools, and with it an apparent impossibility of answering the appeal without specializing the work of such candidates if there is to be any hope of success. It may be that many a school owes its position and success to the development of these many sides; but we are only just beginning to realize not only the drain it makes upon resources and the difficulties that may arise in the future, but the change it brings about in the very nature of the schoolmaster's profession. It is not enough to say that organizing means the arrangement of a time-table that will work ; it implies personal contact with many branches of class-room life, personal supervision, and perpetual interruption from outside.

Secondly, circumstances have produced in many of the activities of English life a strong tendency to 'professionalize'; we may call it, if we like, the raising of the standard owing to general competition. At any rate, not a whit less in schools than elsewhere has the tendency made itself felt. In its more oppressive form it shows itself in marking off special departments of school life. To excel in any one of these requires perhaps special concentration ; and excellence in any special department is held to be a sufficient excuse for weakness or failure elsewhere. It is instructive sometimes in this connexion to read the list of 'Honours' recited on Speech Days. Not less 'professional,' or, if we please to modify the term, not less 'special,' is the work required or imposed in the preparation of Sixth Form boys for University distinctions. It is true that the work has been begun in the private schools; and any one who has examined little boys under fourteen for entrance scholarships must have been amazed at the skill which they have been trained to display in the art of doing examination papers. But though the Universities or any other body of brain purchasers desire or strive to make their examinations general, to encourage sound learning, to insist upon promise and general ability more than upon actual performance or special cunning, yet ultimately the conditions of the competition produce a set of picked boys, who are entrusted to a young scholar fresh from the University examinations and inspired by the teaching of those who will examine for College scholarships; he is often made to feel that it is his business to see that a certain proportion of scholarships shall be obtained, and he knows that the criterion of ability in his candidate will be the promise of a First in the University examinations. We are examination-ridden, and the condemnation or approval of such a system depends entirely upon the motives for learning and the character of the examination. But at least it is admitted that this special work demands the special attention and is to a great extent the *raison d'être* of the Sixth Form Tutor.

Although these circumstances are sufficient to account for the importance of his position and the increased responsibilities imposed upon him, there is yet another characteristic element in public school life

with which he is immediately brought into contact—
the Prefect system. The rights as well as the duties
of prefects and Sixth Form boys place them above
the law which affects inferior mortals. If their
teacher is compelled to enforce discipline, it must
be by other means and under a different sanction.
In truth there is very little to distinguish the
methods of dealing with Sixth Form boys at school
and with undergraduates at the University, partly, it
may be, because undergraduates are treated more
like boys, but chiefly because boys have been given
in a very much larger degree the liberties of undergraduates. It was seen from the first that the only
hope of success in carrying out such a system of
self-government, in reposing trust where treachery
means incalculable mischief, was sympathy and
friendliness between master and boy, the appeal to
reason rather than force. It is then the business of
the Sixth Form Tutor—nay, it is his only chance
in the large boarding schools and in any of the day
schools where the prefect system is effective—to
know his prefects as a friend and a brother.

And as the area and scope of the education of
Sixth Form boys has been altered, so its aspect
has in the last generation been materially changed.
The old lines of Grammar and Rhetoric have been
removed ; or perhaps it would be better to say that
the old tradition of basing the study of the Classics
upon Grammar and cultivating the elements of
Rhetoric has gone. Nowadays no one expects

Sixth Form boys to be able to repeat *verbatim* the pages of a grammar; it is very rare to find them regularly learning by heart large masses of the authors they are reading; the practice of original composition is almost entirely confined to annual competition for a prize, and the dilemma in which the head-masters find themselves in trying to make the competition really useful is notorious. For most of these old-fashioned luxuries we are always told there is no time. The claims of other branches of learning and other interests must be allowed. History and English Literature, for instance, find now a regular place in many time-tables of Sixth Form work, and the lectures upon these subjects are perhaps the most advanced and elaborate they hear; whereas in the old days boys were expected to work the subjects out for themselves, and, if they offered them for examination, offered them on their own responsibility and independently. And so too in the study of classical books; there is a great amount of careful preparation; the bulk and number of commentaries have enormously increased, and the evisceration of these has produced a mass of school editions which too often do duty for the intelligent use of a dictionary and take the place of independent thought. But at the same time it must be allowed that there is a certain amount of what may be called more cursory reading, done by boys either independently or in Form without any view to an examination.

It is probably not worth while, even if it were possible, to answer the question whether more or less is actually read by a Sixth Form now than was read thirty or forty years ago ; but in comparing the work of the two periods two points of importance, which are at the same time indisputable, emerge : first, that far more actual teaching is expected and is given ; secondly, that the system is thoroughly democratic—that is, on the whole the standard of expectation is what the mediocre or ordinary boy can do. On both sides, the serious danger of evil consequences to education has been created perhaps by the lengths to which we have carried the system of competitive examination ; the danger, on the one side, of over-teaching created by the feverish desire to present immediately striking and successful results ; the danger, on the other side, of cheapening the effort required of the cleverer boys by putting nothing out of the reach of the dullest. In the curriculum of work this principle has brought about an elaborate scheme of alternative subjects, and it is often decided for a boy, oftener perhaps by the boy, long before he arrives at the Sixth Form, that he shall be allowed to drop one subject for which he is fancied to have no turn and to take up another which will be more profitable to him. It is ridiculous of course to suppose that every boy has the same turn or even any taste, say, for writing Latin verses ; it is only common sense to cast about and see how he may spend his time more profitably ; the point, however, that may easily be overlooked, but should, it seems to me, be secured before all others, is that the effort and discipline demanded by the alternative subject shall be really serious. The complexity of subjects produced by this system, the consequent difficulty in many schools of providing adequately for the alternatives, and the frailties of human nature seen in the motives which decide the value of a particular study to a particular boy—all these combine to introduce an element of danger into what is at first sight, and obviously is in its nature, calculated to be a useful and happy development. There is a danger of watering down the methods of study to the incapacities of the weaker brother and of yielding inconsiderately to impatient outcry raised from outside. One of the immediate difficulties which the multifarious aspect of Sixth Form teaching presents arises out of a difference of view under which the several parts of the work are presented, and a difference in the necessities imposed by circumstance upon the boys themselves. Happy should be the head-master who has no boy in his Sixth who is compelled to obtain a scholarship somewhere ! Happy, but for comparative tables of results, and the almost insurmountable difficulty of stimulating ambition and a spirit of hard work without such necessities ! And the diversity of view with which different lessons are regarded has a tendency to consign to the classroom the less advanced parts of Sixth Form work, to take away from the importance of those subjects which are not to be offered for examination or are taken up by weaker brethren *pour passer le temps*, and to lay special emphasis upon the higher work done by a select few who are to win distinction in examinations.

And yet there is, I suppose, some fundamental idea underlying the methods and aims of those who teach a Sixth Form now and have deliberately abandoned the old lines; it is perhaps something in the way of cultivating fluency, not in composition so much as in reading and understanding a dead or a foreign language, and this as a means for quickening the intelligence and stimulating thought as well as literary interest. We are perhaps nowadays more concerned, at school, about the thought and meaning of the author than about the form in which they are presented. The question then arises, may we not be stultifying our own purpose by abandoning many devices useful enough, if not indeed necessary, for enabling us to produce a freer familiarity with those languages? And are we not often imposing upon boys of seventeen or eighteen those methods which are only useful to us at the end of a University career? Composition, for instance—verse composition at any rate—and repetition are more or less discredited tasks; and yet few will deny that it is easier to read and appreciate the force of a Greek or Latin poet after training and practice in their metres. Again, there is no need to keep composition within the narrow grooves in which it now runs; the retranslation into the original of large masses of the prose authors that are being read, especially if the English for retranslation is carefully prepared and represents a definite style, cannot fail to produce confidence and a greater certainty in seeing the author's meaning than almost any other method yet devised. M. Riemann, in his Introduction to *Études sur la langue et la grammaire de Tite Live*, has stated the issue most clearly when he says: 'Il est vrai que, lorsqu'on étudie une langue morte, le but qu'on se propose est simplement de la savoir lire; mais on ne sait une langue, morte ou vivante, que si on est en état de l'écrire à peu près correctement, et, pour arriver à comprendre les auteurs latins, il faut s'être exercé à écrire et à penser dans leur langue.'

Or again, if any one is rash enough to make such a reactionary proposal as to revive repetition in full force, it need not mean a parrot-like performance of so many lines reeled off like 'a tale told by an idiot, signifying nothing'; it is just as easy to devise passages of repetition from the best parts of the authors with whom the Form is already becoming familiar. It would indeed seem easier to make repetition useful as a means of mastering a language as well as of stimulating literary interest with Sixth Forms than with any lower Form; and yet this is just the place in the school where the practice is usually dropped.

And once again, the study of grammar—especially

the syntax of the language—has been largely abandoned in Sixth Form teaching; partly because the
old-fashioned practice of committing to memory and
repeating pages of a standard grammar seemed
profitless and to many a waste of time; partly because it has been felt that for examination purposes
the results are satisfactory neither to examiners nor
to teachers: the answers to grammar questions too
often reduce themselves to a bald and servile repro-
duction of the notes given in the class-room—a performance even more self-condemned than the old
form of repetition—and the teacher finds either that
the subject is crowded out or that he must practically
begin at the beginning of all things. If he can feel
the *robur et aes triplex* about his heart and boldly
begins, his position may become more perplexing
than ever; for the study of syntax has been practically reserved for the Sixth Form, and so the new
arrivals know nothing of the subject, whilst the old
hands may have begun to grasp its principles and
meaning. I do not think there is any exaggeration
in saying that a thorough study of Greek and Latin
syntax and a real grip of the idiom of the language
are not to be found in the Sixth Forms of our public
schools. Boys who are being trained to get scholarships have some kind of special teaching in it, but as
a rule only in the way of the notes already mentioned:
and the Form as a whole acquires a certain facility
by constant practice in 'Unseen Translation'; but
the study of grammar, as grammar, has gone. And

yet again here it is admitted that we have deliberately abandoned means for stimulating thought as serviceable to school-boys as logic is to undergraduates, and as interesting as any other part of the study of the Greek and Latin languages; interesting, that is, not only to the specialist, but to any intelligent boy who is made to see the kinds of ways in which the idioms and structure of a language have been formed and developed, what is the logic underlying them, and how they compare with the syntax of a kindred language. But as a question of practical politics, a systematic study of the subject is generally regarded as impossible, simply on the ground of want of time—I am speaking particularly of the case of our boarding schools—and the only course open is to make school lessons, which consist chiefly of the translation of Greek and Latin authors, as real and interesting as possible from the literary point of view, trusting that a smattering of grammatical knowledge and criticism will be picked up by the way.

Here we are at once face to face with the democratic principle entering into education ; what seems at first sight more useful—or perhaps what is demanded as more useful—by the majority is accepted as the standard and rule. In this particular instance it is very doubtful whether an education from the literary point of view is the most useful for anything like the number of boys upon whom it is imposed. However, when we begin to treat of literary interest, we are treading upon dangerous ground. The effort to stimulate literary interest amongst boys with regard to their school-work, to induce masters to make their teaching interesting and inspired with life, is the characteristic feature of public school teaching, particularly in the higher parts of a school, at this time ; indeed, when the methods suggested for giving practical training to teachers in secondary schools are analyzed, it is generally found that they amount almost entirely to this. This effort is truly a wholesome and inevitable protest against the dry manners and stiff pedantry of the old-fashioned pedagogue, as well as against the spirit of 'cram' which our examination systems produce. As far as Sixth Form teaching is concerned, it has en-abled one great difficulty which meets head-masters to be partly solved — the difficulty, when Sixth Form boys are separated by the sharp divisions of different sides or departments, of getting them together in a body for at any rate some part of their school work ; for the handling of any author, English, French, German, Greek, or Latin, from this point of view will within limits serve a purpose useful to all, and alone make Form teaching for a class of combined Sixth Form boys possible.

But when all admit so much, it is at least open to question whether we are altogether judicious in the way this principle of teaching is being enforced. In the first place we are, by the incessant talk about literary interest, easily apt to make it repulsive or else to foster incorrigible priggishness. It is, I suppose, within the experience of most men of education and culture that the capacity for literary criticism and even for appreciation is generally the last faculty developed; boys, and even men, know when a book or a passage in an author appeals to them without in the least being able to analyze the cause. Even if we grant that they ought to be able, it is extremely doubtful whether a prevailing method of spooning literary jargon into their mouths will serve the end in view. A teacher of Sixth Form boys had the opportunity from time to time of reading aloud to them passages of English without any comment, and with perhaps only a word of introduction to explain the context; there was no knowing what would appeal to most boys, or even the best boys. As a matter of fact, the passage that apparently produced most impression and excited the largest number of questions was Jowett's translation of the closing paragraphs of the *Republic*. And it must be clear to any one who has made such experiments or, feeling a literary interest himself, has interpreted an author to boys in the ordinary way of lessons in class, that he is likely to stifle original or independent thought and to sicken his pupils of genuine enthusiasm, if literary appreciations are forced down their throats. Though this must be obvious, yet it is a point to be insisted upon in view of the mass of school editions—many of them adapted for the use of the lower forms—which are filled with literary comment, possessing perhaps some autobiographical interest to the editor, but only reproduced in examinations by the learners *verbatim* without real intelligence. Those who teach and those who examine must all be aware of the lengths to which this system has been carried. The exaggeration of it is seen not only in the amount of such teaching applied to the highest forms, but in the extent to which it is carried down into the lower parts of a school. We are riding our hobby to death, and often seem to forget that it is just the variety in capacities and interests of teachers and the methods employed by them which has produced, it may be quite unconsciously, some of the most useful results in the educational work of a public school. It is quite reasonable to maintain that even the dullest and driest teacher has in his place done not less useful work than any of his liveliest colleagues. The truth is that much, perhaps most, of what is stigma- tized as bad teaching is due to the lack of interest and energy in self-education and self-improvement upon the part of the teacher. Of all the essentials for acquiring the power to impart knowledge—par- ticularly to Sixth Form boys—the most conspicuous, it seems to me, is intellectual self-improvement. Of the personal qualities which already imply that power, and can never be imparted, nothing need be said ; but it is too true that many a teacher remains satisfied with the modicum of knowledge he acquired at the University, and men are often chosen to instruct even the best boys in a public school because of qualifications almost inconsistent with a real interest in learning.

But though some of the problems here suggested are important enough, and deserve serious consideration, they raise, comparatively speaking, but minor difficulties. The chief difficulties to be met in carrying out the education of a Sixth Form arise out of the situation now found existing in our public boarding schools. First of all, the attitude of the English public towards our large boarding schools has altered very materially. There is a very widespread feeling amongst all kinds and classes of persons in favour of giving a boy a public school education; the result is the old schools are full to overflowing, and many new schools have come into being and are often as crowded as the old, and more ready to grow larger. With this almost universal feeling has come the demand for many different kinds of education. The demand may have created the supply or the supply the demand. The result is that there is an effort to keep up the best traditions of the old gregarious form of school life, to educate *en masse*, and at the same time an effort to be elastic, and take account of and provide for a variety of careers. Now the very essence of public school life has been the system of self-government in the hands of Prefects, and the difficult problem—a problem which promises to press even more heavily in the future—is, Can this be carried on, when success in examinations is the criterion of industry and sometimes the only reason for the popularity of a school, and when special training or 'cramming' is necessary to ensure this success? The plain question is, 'Will the Prefect system have to go?' The calls upon the time and attention of a Prefect in a public school are as clearly defined as they are numerous; they are the regular days of 'duty,' preserving law and order in the house during preparation and other times; the active sup-port of school institutions, such as literary and debating and other societies, or editing the school journal. In the modern professionalizing of athletics, if he be captain of any game—sometimes it is enough if he be one of the representatives—his attention to school work will be nominal, and his position with its duties is held by parents as well as masters to be sufficient excuse for failure in school work. It is true that a kind of compromise has been effected in the solu-tion of this difficulty. It is a common practice now-adays to select the head of a school from among the body of Prefects irrespective of his place in the Sixth, and to make Prefects of boys of character and leading, more or less irrespective of their place in the school. The practice has grown out of the recognition of qualities other than intellectual superiority, and it seems to carry with it the practical advantage of relieving what we may call the working Sixth of many of its cares. This however is no real reconcilia-tion of the conflicting interests in the public schools of to-day. It emphasizes the sharp division between workers and players, between the student and the boy of action ; and in the long run learning suffers, even if it is not degraded. Intellectual interest and the love of true learning hold the awkward place in a triangular duel ; they are exposed to the attack of the craze for athletics on one side and of cram for examinations on another. It is easy and common enough to adopt a cheery optimism ; to say that somehow things right themselves ; that the true love of learning is found in our schools, and in some way receives more encouragement than before. It may also be impossible and therefore unnecessary to reconcile fully the conflict of interests ; and it would not perhaps be difficult to show that the English people, in having to choose one side, have always preferred the education which forms character to that which fosters learning. We never tire of repeating that Waterloo was won on the playing-fields of Eton. But while all this may be cheerfully admitted, we are still leaving out of account some of the most serious points for reflection. The born student, it is true, can be left to take care of himself; but what of the average Sixth Form boy whose instincts are half-formed and untrained? What effect will it have upon the mass to raise false standards and to allow meaner and more trivial aims to be the objects of existence? And if the purpose of public school education with us is above all and at all costs to form character, what is the character which our present system is actually stamping upon men? We are a long way from Waterloo, and English tempera-

ment and character have been and still are under-
going many striking changes ; are the qualities which
are now developing amongst us all, and not least
among our public school men, the qualities which
win ?

But even apart from the consideration of modern
tendencies on what may be called their moral side,
we cannot fail to notice the fundamental change which
has been made in our attitude towards the problem
of education in its relation directly to the intellect :
modern education insists upon many subjects being
taught to as large a number of boys as possible, and
the principle upon which this demand rests is utilitarian.   But we have yet to be told what becomes of
all these subjects in the history of a particular boy,
and from the utilitarian point of view what positive
purpose the teaching of them has served as compared
with a system of education whose one aim is to train
the intellect and open the mind.

H. M. BURGE.

SIXTH FORM TEACHING IN A DAY SCHOOL

'Es bildet ein Talent sich in der Stille,
Sich ein Charakter in dem Strom der Welt.'

THE question of the comparative merits of the education obtainable respectively in day schools and in boarding schools has attracted of late a good deal of attention. An exhaustive discussion of the subject, however important—and there are few educational questions of greater importance—is no part of the object of this essay. But in dealing with the teaching of the highest classical forms from the point of view of one whose experience has been wholly in a day school, it is impossible not to begin by asking what it is that constitutes the essential difference, if such there be, between the two types.

In the course of the last thirty years the great day schools of the country have at least proved that from the purely intellectual side they are able to give an education which need not fear comparison with the best results obtained by the training of a boarding school. The Schools Inquiry Commission of 1868 unhesitatingly reported that the boarding school was

F

not merely better for the formation of character, but was also the more efficient instrument of teaching (vol. i. p. 44). Yet even in 1868 there was evidence that the latter half of this statement was by no means a necessary truth, and nowadays it might almost be regarded as something of the nature of a paradox. Whether the former half still remains as true as it undoubtedly was at the time is an interesting question, with which however this paper can only deal incidentally. It may be confessed that in the matter of formation of character the day schools as such have still a heavy task before them — a task however which, for my own part, I do not consider by any means hopeless. But without going into this matter, it is worth while to consider briefly what are the causes and conditions which have made the present state of things possible. Considerable misapprehension exists on the subject. On the one hand, it is not true that the public boarding schools as a whole have ceased to teach anything but cricket and football; on the contrary, their standard of work is probably as high and their standard of teaching considerably higher now than it ever was before. On the other hand, it is not true that the day schools have deliberately sacrificed the ultimate interest of their pupils—physical, mental, and moral—for the sake of immediate success or vulgar advertisement. The advantages which a day school admittedly possesses are rather to be sought in permanent conditions of their existence— conditions which have been further developed by the fact that those social and economical forces which are specially favourable to a day-school education—in a word, the increasing poverty of the professional classes—have been specially active at a time when the fortunes of the great public day schools have been in the hands of men of exceptional ability.

Various other answers have been given to the question, none of which seem to me to have more than a contributory value. The day schools are supposed to have unrivalled facilities for going into the market and purchasing scholars. It is true that in the case of one prominent school the number of scholars on the foundation is a quarter of the whole number of boys in the school. It is also true, as I believe, that that number might be reduced by half without the success of the school being necessarily affected ; and whether this is so or not, it is plain that the explanation will not apply to the cases of Merchant Taylors' and Manchester. And though no doubt the low scale of tuition fees which obtains at many day schools in itself constitutes a 'bribe' analogous to that offered by foundation scholarships, this fact in itself is hardly adequate to account for the whole result. It is also said that the cause is to be sought in the comparative poverty of the boys, which leads them from an early age to consider prudential motives. As a matter of fact, the class of society from which most of the London day schools draw their pupils does not probably differ very much from the class that sends its boys to

Marlborough or Haileybury.   But apart from this, it is surely too much to ask even of a London boy to regard his education from the first as an investment. These prudential considerations may appeal to boys of sixteen and upwards, but unless habits of industry are formed long before that age, it will be too late in ordinary cases for ultimate success.   Again, it is argued that the town boy is naturally brighter and more intelligent than the country boy.   This, even if true, is only a partial explanation.   Probably the best material in the kingdom is to be found in those boys— many of them sons of the country clergy — who win places on the foundations of Winchester and Eton.   And it must not be forgotten that the country schools get at least their fair share of town boys. The population of London alone is five millions; only a small percentage of its boys are to be found in its day schools.   The fact is that there are poor boys and clever boys in the country schools as well.   The boy of really first-class ability will succeed wherever he goes; and it may be admitted for the sake of argument that he is more common in a day school than in a boarding school, or is less liable there to run to seed.   Any school may be thankful for such boys, but it can hardly take full credit to itself for them.   The standard by which alone it can be fairly judged is the degree of its success with the ordinarily intelligent boys and its absolute success or failure with wholly unpromising material.   Lastly, it is alleged that the success of the day schools is due to their sacrificing the future to the present, to their neglecting the most important elements of a generous and rational system of education, while hunting for scholarships as a professional athlete hunts for prizes. But even so, the question still remains how the ordinary boy comes to submit himself to this régime.

I am very far from denying that there is an element of truth in all the suggested reasons, but they seem to me in no case to be the essential cause, and neither individually nor conjointly to account for the facts. The simple truth is that the day boy lives at home. I am not concerned here with what he loses by so doing, and he loses much; the point is what he gains. First of all he gains in most cases the constant interest of his parents in his work. His evening lessons become a permanent feature in the family life; domestic arrangements are made with reference to them; his daily experiences are a matter of family interest; his father or elder brother will often concern himself personally in his work. The clever boy, who generally comes of an intelligent family, has the daily stimulus of intellectual sympathy, and need not cultivate his literary tastes in holes and corners to avoid attracting notice. The poor widow's son has the necessity of application kept daily before him, and learns not to be ashamed of his poverty. The masters often become friends of the household. In any case it is not so easy for a boy to be going from bad to worse all the term and his parents to remain in ignorance of it. On the other hand, the evil influence of the idle boy does not extend every evening to thirty or forty other boys in his own house.

There is of course another side to all this. School-masters as a class suffer much from parents, and the master in a day school most of all. The parent may be a doctrinaire—there are many such nowadays—and all his interests in his son, often acute enough, may be directed on other lines, supplementary or antagonistic to the school teaching. Or the parents may go much into society, and either leave their son to the charge of the butler and housekeeper or take him themselves into surroundings where he becomes a young man about town before his time. There is a peculiar type of boy who comes to school from the London suburbs that many masters will recognize. Other parents again, from a mistaken sense of duty, will encourage a boy to spend his evenings in various forms of philanthropic or religious work, and music also claims many victims. But taken as a whole, the sympathy and interest of the parent is the day-school master's strongest support ; without it his work would generally be in vain. And even in cases where the parents are weak or indifferent, a boy may learn an amount of independence and self-reliance from the mere absence of external aid, which he often fails to learn at a boarding school, or even at the University.

Another advantage, particularly in the highest forms of a school, which follows from the fact that a boy lives at home, is that his time out of school is not so entirely taken up with matters

of school and house management as is too often the
case with the Sixth Form boy in a boarding house.
I should be the last person in the world to undervalue the advantages of the monitorial system as it
affects Sixth Form boys themselves no less than as
an instrument of government. The fact however
remains that the more conscientious a praepostor,
the less time he has to himself outside his form
room. It is not, I believe, rare for such a boy
deliberately to sacrifice his own work, about which
in itself he may be eager enough, for the sake of
some duty, disciplinary or athletic, which seems at
the time to have, in the strictest sense of the words,
higher claims. Even if this is an exaggerated statement, at least the day boy is free from such distractions. The monitorial system does indeed exist in
some day schools, but can never have the same
position there as in a boarding school, where after
all it is the management of the boarding house that
is the exacting charge. The day boy loses much,
very much, by the absence of what many men would
regard as the most valuable part of their education;
but the extent of his loss need not be exaggerated.
Since Arnold's time, in the hands of a series of wise
head-masters, the monitorial system has come to be
a most valuable part of our public school organization: in some schools it was possibly such at an
earlier date. But it is perhaps—though I hesitate
to say it—not the essential part, and the virtues
characteristic of public school men are, I believe,

obtainable, though not so easily, nor perhaps to the same extent, without it. And even now it is not free from abuses. It has lent itself to the modern craze for athleticism in a not altogether creditable degree. The leading athletes nowadays in most schools are also the leading monitors, and they are so too often in virtue solely of their athletic prestige. If they were not admitted into the official hierarchy, they would set up one of their own, which the school at large would recognize as the more legitimate. But it is a dangerous policy to call in the barbarians for the protection of the empire. Moreover, by hook or by crook, some of them must be got up into the Sixth. I once knew a schoolmaster who, having in his form the captain of the Eleven, got him through the term on an average of marks proportionate to his average for the time being with bat and ball. I do not say that this was not as good as any other method; it served the required purpose; but such a case gives away the whole situation. And once in the Sixth, either they must be frankly allowed to do nothing, or in the effort to get something into their heads the better boys must be sacrificed [1].

[1] It is no part of the purpose of this essay to suggest a remedy for the state of things described, but it might perhaps be sought in the direction of a reduction of the number of boys in a boarding house. If the maximum were twenty instead of forty or even seventy, the responsibilities of the Sixth Form would be greatly reduced ; the gap between the athlete and the student would be narrowed, a larger proportion of boys being in their house athletic teams; the house-

Now the athletics of day schools are often quite sufficiently good, and the interest taken in them quite great enough, to promote the cardinal virtues. Boys living in a great town are not likely to live entirely outside the influence of special editions of the evening papers. But the exigencies of the situation do not require the school to be organized from the point of view of athletics or of house government. It is possible to have your head form free of honorary members, and it is possible to get the clever boys there young. It is also possible to suggest subjects for private reading or special work, knowing that the boys have no prior claims on their spare time. I am not blind to the dangers of turning out a set of prigs, to the evils of intellectual arrogance, of selfishness and individualism that may result. I would only say that I believe that these dangers may be overcome, that the teacher has the matter very much in his own hands, and that the London boy at any rate generally has too much *savoir faire* to be a prig of the worst type. That such boys may be healthy, honest, vigorous boys, loyal to their school and to one another, I have abundant proof. The particular knowledge of human nature and sense of responsibility that at other schools is got by the exercise of delegated authority, is got by them in some degree at any

master would be able to know something individually of his boys; and the prospects of promotion on the staff of the school would be doubled. I recognize obvious counterbalancing disadvantages.

rate in other ways, from the mere fact that their school-fellows represent types very much more diverse than is the case in the country schools, and that the elder boys are the guardians of the good name of the school, if not so much in the school itself, at least in the street and train.

And this brings me to another point. It is a common matter of remark that what is called the 'public school system' tends to exterminate individuality. Each school prides itself on turning out a particular stamp of boy; and how successful they are in doing so every college tutor knows. The types are very different, and most of them very excellent, but they are types. That something is lost by this, every serious investigator of the subject must admit. It is, on the other hand, perhaps the chief privilege of a day school that it can recognize and encourage very diverse forms of excellence. Enough indeed is not done in this matter. Every day-school master must have known boys who possessed a really astonishing knowledge of some out-of-the-way subject acquired in spare time and quite spontaneously. Not long ago a boy from a London school was given a scholarship at a Cambridge College on his knowledge of Assyrian cuneiform inscriptions, and similar instances are not rare. You do not want all your boys to be pedants; you do want to secure that a special aptitude or taste for a particular branch of learning is not crushed out. We know that Darwin was considered a foolish dreamer at Shrewsbury; he

would have been at least less likely to be so misunder-
stood at a day school.   Every large day school has
its gallery and its museum within reach ; few probably
make much use of them, but it is a matter in which
parents and masters might well co-operate more than
they do, the more so that, as I hope to point out later,
the actual amount of ground that can be covered in
class, at any rate in the top forms of a day school,
is more restricted than in the corresponding part of
a boarding school.

Before going further, one word may be permitted
about the Sixth Form master himself.   It is important
for him to remember that, as will be shown further
on, he will want all his time.   Let him therefore waste
none.   Marks and form orders may be reduced to a
minimum or altogether done away with ; the stimulus
they give will be easily dispensed with, the labour they
entail is often enormous.   Examinations may also be
discarded.   There will be the midsummer visit of
the external examiner, which will have a certain value
of its own for the form as a whole, and the shadow of
the college scholarship examinations will be always
across the path.   No others are necessary, though
some may be inevitable.   The master will want his
time for teaching and for his own private reading ; if
for no other reason than that he must keep himself
up to the mark.   He has to convince his boys of
the reality and the progressive character of classical
scholarship; and the more he continues to learn
himself, the more minute his acquaintance even with

an outlying branch of learning, the better will be his work. He has to deal with boys some of whom in intellectual vigour may be among the best of their generation ; he must recognize their claims, and even their superiority. If he has been openly confuted by one of his own pupils on a point of scholarship, he may consider the defeat a victory, but he must have proved a worthy antagonist. He will thus find plenty of occupation for his spare hours, whether in term-time or in the holidays.

His pupils will be boys of all ages from nineteen to fifteen ; of very varying tastes and very varying ability, but all of them with at least a reasonable amount of industry, without which, save in exceptional cases, they would not have got to that part of the school. There need be, as we have seen, no honorary members of the form ; for the rest, the causes already indicated will have provided a sufficient number of industrious boys in the school to secure the survival of the fittest. The master will hope to find that these boys have been soundly grounded in the principles of grammar and syntax at an earlier stage in their career, and that they have not forgotten them, as too often happens, in their progress up the school. He will also hope that they have been taught these principles in a rational, scientific, and scholarly way. It would be long to explain what precisely this implies, but the main point is that there should be as little to unteach as possible. He will probably find that all the boys are hoping to proceed to the Universities, and possibly that all hope to get scholarships or exhibitions: the majority because they cannot go up without one, the small minority from an emulation not necessarily of an ungenerous kind. To the former class at any rate he will feel a grave sense of responsibility, knowing what their failure means. About the cleverer boys he may be comparatively at his ease, knowing, as he soon will, that they will teach themselves, or, what is equally important, teach one another. They will be his most interesting, and he will be right in considering them his most important pupils ; for it is in the best interests not merely of the school but of the country at large that the claims of quality should be considered paramount. There is probably no more pernicious doctrine among educationalists, popular as it is nowadays, than that it is the duty of the schoolmaster to reach a good average. But the teaching of clever boys is its own reward ; it is with the less able but not less deserving boys that the work will sometimes seem oppressive, and the reward, at any rate in the form of material success, slow to come.

The number of boys in his form will, it is hoped, be small—not more than eighteen or twenty—and this for two reasons. In the first place, the greater individuality of the day boy, of which I have already spoken, and which will be most pronounced in this part of the school, will make it difficult for him to do justice to the form *en bloc,* and will necessitate a good deal of individual attention. But there is a practical difficulty which makes a small form even more necessary. The whole of the work with the boys, including the looking over of compositions, will have to be done in some twenty-five weekly hours spent in school, or, allowing for a certain number of hours given to other subjects, in even less time. The Sixth Form master in a boarding school generally sees his boys for composition, &c., individually out of school; in a day school this is impossible. No one who has not tried it knows what this means. Allowing four pieces of written work a week to a form of eighteen boys, and giving each boy only ten minutes at a time—and little good can be done in less—this comes to twelve hours a week, that is, nearly half of the whole available number. The pieces will also have been looked over privately by the master beforehand, so that, allowing an additional five minutes of this process for each copy, in ten years he may expect to spend something like three hundred days of twenty-four hours each in looking over composition. This is not a light task, and is pleasanter in the retrospect than in the prospect. It will of course be objected that in allowing so much time for this subject, I am attaching a preposterous importance to what is often described as at best a mere piece of trickery. My answer would be that the master's first business is to make his boys good classical scholars, and that composition is the best, if not the only means to that end. Into the merits of the question it is impossible here to enter: I merely give my conviction based upon ten years' experience with some 125 boys for what it may be worth. It is at any rate plain that with more than some eighteen boys in a form, the system, such as it is, would become unworkable.

On the teaching of composition there is not much to be said. The main point is to be as definite as possible, and it is possible to be much more definite than is generally believed. The ordinary handbooks are excellent, and the master will possess them and perhaps use them himself, but he will not recommend them to his boys; partly because, if he did, they would not read them (nor indeed is the best of them exhilarating reading), partly because all teaching of composition must be so individual a thing as between pupil and master that it cannot be done vicariously. 'Fair copies' are generally dictated or distributed. but I doubt whether in this shape they are much good, though they come in usefully in later years, when the pupil becomes a teacher, and it is probably not till then that most boys ever look at them again. A far better way is for the master, having written his own version or perhaps studied more or less the version in the key, to get his form to make their own, inviting suggestions, incorporating the best phrases in the copies shown up, accepting alternatives, and so forth. Such viva voce composition, perhaps supplemented by the final dictation of the fair copy, enables common mistakes to be insisted on once for all, warnings to be given against errors which only one boy has made but which others would have made if they had had the opportunity, and generally saves time in the long run. The method might probably be employed with special effect in verse composition, but the master will probably find that he has not got the time, even if he has the courage.

A variety of styles is not to be encouraged. Cicero and Virgil are probably sufficient models for Latin. The subject-matter of Cicero is varied enough for all practical purposes ; Caesar and Livy are not familiar authors at that stage in a schoolboy's life, and the style of Tacitus, for all its excellence, is as little a model of normal Latin as is the style of Apuleius. About Virgil there will be no question. The modern Latin elegiac has no classical models ; indeed it is probably the nearest approach to original composition in a dead language to which most of us attain, and it must be treated as such. Ovid is plainly no pattern for the translation of *In Memoriam.*

In Greek the question is more complicated, if only because there we are dealing with the language of a people with whom style was instinctive and instinctively correlated to the subject-matter. Cicero was taught to write Latin in a sense in which not even the pupils of Isocrates were taught to write Greek. Here Plato, the greatest of them all, is essential ; so is Thucydides ; Demosthenes perhaps in a less degree. Sophocles must be held up as the unattainable model for verse ; Euripides is often merely 'tricky,' and he would be a bold man who should encourage his pupils to 'hew a colossus out of the rock' with the chisel of Aeschylus.

But indeed it is more important to insist on grammatical and syntactical accuracy than on style, and inasmuch as grammar and syntax differ at different periods of a language, the master will probably find his hands full enough in teaching those of the best period properly, while a boy in learning what is not Ciceronian may learn incidentally what is Tacitean. Style is a matter rather of inoculation than of inculcation and will develop more or less of itself, though books like Nägelsbach's *Stylistik* are useful, if rather unmanageable. But above all things the composition should be brought into close relation with the Greek and Latin authors that are being read in form. This is where, as I venture to think, composition masters as such find their hands tied, as college tutors certainly do. Re-translation of a free rendering of a passage of the current prose author is often valuable, especially with younger boys.

I do not wish to enter here on the vexed question of verse-writing. In a form of the kind I have described, most, at any rate, of the boys will write verses. I wish however to record my conviction that verse-writing, both in Greek and Latin, is an unrivalled instrument for the development of all the

G

higher qualities of the scholar, and not less valuable as teaching a proper insight into and appreciation of modern poetry.   And when boys have reached such a stage of development as to be on the threshold of the highest form, I see no reason why they should drop the practice, just at the moment when in both respects it is likely to be most beneficial.

A construing lesson is pretty much the same all the world over.   Yet even in Sixth Forms it is too often merely a dismal hammering out of the daily quota of lines which the boys are supposed to have prepared and the master thinks himself bound to get through in a given time.   Such a lesson ought to be a systematic but sympathetic reading of the literature of a language.   This ideal is perhaps never attained and never attainable, but possibly one or two suggestions based on actual experience may be permitted. In the first place, it is not necessary to prescribe the daily tale of bricks.   It should be generally understood that the boys are expected to have got up a reasonable amount, but to insist on so many lines is putting a wrong complexion on the case from the first; and further, if you insist, you have to see that you get them.   Next, it is very desirable, as has always been felt, that an author should, if possible, be read in bulk.   It is not every author that can be so treated, but if it is possible for six books of Virgil or twelve books of Homer to be got through in a term, something has been done towards that end.   Now, in the first place, an author should be read continuously:

the plan by which two or three different authors, sometimes assigned to different masters, are kept going at the same time, each author with three or four hours a week allowed him, means considerable waste of time and dissipation of effort. But by going on continuously with a dozen books of Homer till they are finished, the boys get to know something of Homer as a whole and will come to be able to get through him easily at the rate of 150 lines an hour. It is also, I think, important to be able to devote a good deal of time at any one sitting to translation, or indeed to any other subject that may be in hand. The ordinary hour of form work is rarely an hour of sixty minutes : what with settling down to the work and winding it up and interruptions for parenthetical remarks, it often comes dangerously near to thirty minutes. If instead of five hours on a whole school-day devoted to five different subjects, there are three periods devoted to three subjects, the boys have some time to learn and the masters to teach, and the subject has some chance of being regarded in its entirety. Even under these conditions it is still necessary that the ground should be quickly covered. To this end it is necessary to put on only or principally the better boys. The weaker do not, I think, really suffer by the seeming neglect : it is easy by other means to find out whether they are doing the work of the form or not, and the power of viva voce translation is not in itself so important as to make it necessary to torture and irritate every one concerned by listening to a hopeless duffer. He will be less exasperating on paper and will not waste every one else's time ; and he will not translate on paper any the worse for having heard a passage decently rendered by a better boy rather than having stumbled through it himself. It is, further, probably necessary under the circumstances to allow, or rather recommend, the boys to use translations. This will be anathema to many schoolmasters ; but it may be observed that as in a day school boys will use 'cribs' whether you like it or not, you may as well sanction what you cannot prevent. Further, the modern translation is often a work of art, useful or indispensable as a model of style, and moreover sometimes, as in the case of Jebb's Sophocles, incorporated in an indispensable edition. Nor must it be forgotten that much is saved if a boy takes a passage rightly from the first, and this a translation generally secures. Some boys have a real gift for remembering their own and other people's mistakes, while they are quite unable to remember the correction.

Not every author, it is true, admits of being treated in the way described, nor indeed is a mere facility for reading Thucydides, like Macaulay, in an armchair, the principal thing to aim at. The real intellectual discipline is given by the minute and conscientious study of a text. It is no bad thing to distinguish between the authors read in any one term or year, and along with half the *Aeneid* or half the *Iliad* to take up, for example, the *Agamemnon* to be studied line by line.   Prescribe the best edition, if there is one, but do not insist on it; boys will bring from home editions of every degree of value, and will be able to raise discussions on points of interpretation which will not be unfruitful.   The ordinary German commentaries may well be encouraged, even if the boys do not know the language.   In a few weeks many of them will pick up enough to make out the general meaning of a note.

In selecting the authors to be read, it is not well to go too far afield.   Homer, Sophocles, Thucydides, Plato, Demosthenes in Greek, Cicero, Virgil, Horace in Latin are the best staple commodities: I would add the *Agamemnon*, which if not read at school will probably never be properly read at all.   Keeping mainly to these authors, most of the boys in a year or two will have got through the greater part of Homer and Horace and probably the whole of Virgil. In their private reading they may be encouraged to read other authors; but it is the business of schools to lay the foundations of scholarship and leave the superstructure to the Universities.   Indeed, I have sometimes been tempted to wish that College autho- rities would definitely require a knowledge of Homer and Virgil from candidates for scholarships.   It is no uncommon thing to find boys coming up to the Universities who have tithed the mint, anise, and cummin of Pindar and Propertius, but neglected the weightier matters of the *Odyssey* and the *Aeneid*.

For written unseen translations there will be little

time, and they are not very important. On the other hand, viva voce unseen will occur almost every day, if under no other circumstances, at least when the form gets beyond the limit up to which it may be reasonably expected to have prepared. There is no evil in this, but rather much good. A boy who attains proficiency in viva voce impromptu will not be at a loss in dealing with the same difficulties on paper. In my own experience for some years I never set a written unseen at all, and if it was occasionally difficult to be sure at what point the viva voce unseen began, the result was not as unsatisfactory as at first sight it might appear.

The proper teaching of grammar and syntax I consider to be of primary importance and· the only true foundation of sound scholarship, but the difficulties are very considerable. It is best taught through composition and in connexion with the books read in form. There are few works on the subject that can be cordially recommended. Goodwin is of course indispensable, and Monro's *Homeric Grammar*, the former for constant reference, the latter to be learnt. In Latin the best book has yet to be written, or perhaps never can be[1]. But the method is more important than the instrument, and the proper method is the comparative and historic. The old

[1] I would cordially recommend Riemann's *Syntaxe Latine* (third edition, Paris, Klincksieck 1894) as far the best for its size; though written in French, I have found no difficulty in using it in form.

system was excellent in its day: formulated by Hermann, it became stereotyped in England in the *Public School Latin Primer.* To that we owe, among other things, the long and generally admirably chosen series of technical terms which used to be considered an adequate answer to any syntactical conundrum. Technical terms have their use, but there is nothing that is so liable to be abused. No wonder that grammar and syntax fell into disrepute, when it was thought that ' Ethic Dative' or 'Subjective Genitive' or 'Graecism' would open any lock. But if boys can once be got to understand that the Latin and Greek languages existed before the Latin and Greek grammars, and that the forces that moulded and changed them were at bottom the same forces that are operating at the present moment in their own mother-tongue, then the learning of grammar and syntax need no longer be a descent into a valley of dry bones, but as bracing and stimulating and, to many boys, as interesting an exercise as you can well have. Comparative Philology, in the ordinary sense of the term, is not a suitable subject for schools ; Comparative Syntax, though not under that name, with so much Comparative Accidence as will make it intelligible, is eminently suitable. It does not matter that all that can be regarded as certain on the subject might be written on a single side of a sheet of note-paper ; the point is not that it should be true, but that it should be stimulating. That it cannot be taught dogmatically, and that boys should see for themselves how precarious are its principles and how uncertain its results, is just the most valuable thing about it. They can be taken, as it were, straight into the philological laboratory and see the experiments being made. They cannot be expected, perhaps the master himself cannot be expected, to read Delbrück ; but at least the main principles, as applied to language still only half-developed, are to be found in Monro's *Homeric Grammar*.

As regards the *Realien* of Greek and Latin life, much still remains to be done. I look forward to the time when there will be found in every school, if not attached to every Sixth Form room, a collection of photographs, raised maps, casts, plans, models, &c., small, if necessary, but carefully selected, illustrating the most prominent features in the daily life of the ancients. Schoolmasters are slow to accept new ideas in this direction, and the work done by the Teachers' Guild has not received the support that it deserves. But any schoolmaster might get a lay figure from an artists' colourman and dress it himself as an Homeric warrior or a Roman consul. 'Segnius irritant animos demissa per aurem[1].'

[1] Wykehamists will perhaps pardon me for mentioning here the new Quingentenary Museum at Winchester, which, though not exclusively classical in its scope and admitting no doubt of further additions in this direction, seems to me in its conception and arrangement to be far the best thing of its kind that I have ever seen. The Edinburgh Academy also contains a collection of pictures and plans which is most admirable.

It will of course be asked, But where in all this scheme of work is room to be found for the really important elements in education? What of the teaching of history, ancient and modern; of English literature; of modern languages; of science; of mathematics? The answer is a simple one. Whether the Sixth Form is to specialize entirely on classics is not a question for the Sixth Form master as such. It rests with the higher powers; and as all or most of the boys in the form, as has been already explained, are candidates for scholarships, so long as the colleges require in effect classics only from the candidates, so long are the masters of day schools likely, and under the circumstances almost bound, to specialize in classics. But in the preceding pages it is not necessarily assumed that the whole of a boy's time will be given to classics; hours may be assigned to modern languages or mathematics, but they will not form part of the work of the ordinary form master. And as the Universities in their wisdom have decided that a modicum of mathematics is all that is required for an ideal scheme of education, a school of the type with which we are dealing cannot afford to go behind this. But the case is not quite so bad as at first sight it may seem. In the first place, a good teacher will lose no opportunity of rousing interest or raising a discussion on subjects which may not come within the proper scope of the lesson in hand. There is a danger of wasting time in such matters, but in judicious hands the stimulus to inquiry thus given, even if it affect only one or two boys, may be of immense benefit. Secondly, we have at our disposal the many hours in each week during which the teacher will be occupied in looking over composition. These hours may be employed in many different ways. The boys may be allowed to read privately and without any reference to prospective examinations authors or subjects that fall outside the ordinary curriculum. For this purpose they may well be encouraged to form themselves into small groups of two or three, the members of which will do a great deal, though quite unconsciously, in stimulating each other's interest and in mutual learning and teaching; or they may read history or any other subjects bearing on their work. To have got through in this way some volumes of Mommsen or Grote is a permanent and wide-reaching advantage to a boy. And I venture to think that the teaching of history as a form subject, in ordinary cases, is not much worth the while. About one boy in twenty on an average has a distinct gift for history; the rest can either get it up or else they cannot. In any case it will form a leading subject of the curriculum at the University. And the history lecture is a fine field for the besetting sin of many schoolmasters, who discourse at large with great eloquence and great enthusiasm and think that they have been teaching their boys when they have been only clearing up their own ideas.

Thirdly, there is no reason why the daily round of Greek and Latin composition should not occasionally be varied by an English essay. I would say much more on this subject; for not only is the importance of writing essays the one point on which all educationalists, at any rate in theory, are agreed, but they have a practical value nowadays even at Cambridge. But the question of want of time once more comes in. It is almost impossible to do justice to a careful essay by a clever boy in much less than half an hour, and it is of all his work the part which most demands that justice should be done to it. In a form of eighteen boys therefore there will not be time for many essays in a term. But lastly, it ·must be remembered that a day school proposes to itself a much more limited field of action than a boarding school. The latter professes to do all that is necessary for the education of a boy during the years he is at school: the day school calls in the co-operation of the parent. In the twenty-five hours a week which are alone at its disposal it can only operate within a certain area; the cultivation of a taste for literature and art, for politics, for modern history and modern science, must be left largely to the home and to the holidays. The opportunities in large towns are ample, and the conversation at the family breakfast table is not likely to be so wholly on golf or cricket or fox-hunting as is the case in some country houses. It is not often the case that boys from day schools when they come to the Universities are found to be in-ferior to their contemporaries either in knowledge or in a capacity for learning non-classical subjects: their classical acquirements generally stand them in good stead, and though the curriculum of their schools may be comparatively narrow, they at least escape the curse of Margites, of whom it was said—

πόλλ' ἠπίστατο ἔργα, κακῶς δ' ἠπίστατο πάντα.

One word may be allowed in conclusion on what has been called the Scholarship Question. The rivalry of Universities and of Colleges, however discreditable in itself, is not a matter in which the schoolmaster can directly interfere. My own impression is that it is as unnecessary as it is unseemly. On the one hand, the type of boy that succeeds at Oxford is so different from the type that succeeds at Cambridge that there is very little competition between the two Universities. When a few years ago a leading Cambridge College suddenly put its scholarship examination in the same week as had been for some time occupied by an Oxford group, the first result was that the number of candidates fell to an extraordinarily low figure and the College announced a supplementary examination at a later date. Further, it cannot be seriously maintained, except in the courtesy of a purely academic discussion, that all College scholarships are either equally hard to obtain or equally desirable when won. The best boys, whatever happens, will go to the Colleges with the greatest prestige. The weaker Colleges, by examining earlier in the year, will not as a whole get better boys, but only boys less well prepared, and be proportionately the losers thereby. The actual time at which examinations are held is for a school such as I have described, provided that it is not burdened with close scholarships, a matter of comparative indifference; all boys are the better for a comparatively free time after getting their scholarships which may be devoted to wide general reading: the best boys are probably brought into line again early in the summer term by the competition for leaving exhibitions : the weaker boys have in some cases obtained a considerable stimulus from the mere fact of their success, and in any case it shows a confession of weakness on the part of the schools to say that they cannot keep them in hand when the pressure of an approaching examination is withdrawn. But it is impossible to condemn too strongly what may in all seriousness be called the cruelty of the arrangements—or rather the chaos— of the present year under which practically the whole of the scholarship examinations at both Universities are compressed into some ten weeks ; so that if any unfortunate boy happens to be ill or meet with an accident during that time, his prospects may not improbably be ruined for life.

CHR. COOKSON.

THE TEACHING OF MATHEMATICS

It is impossible in the space of a short essay like this to discuss in detail the questions that arise in connexion with each separate branch of Mathematics, and I shall content myself with mentioning a few points suggested by some experience in teaching not only boys who are taking Mathematics as part of the ordinary school routine, but also those who are doing more advanced work for scholarship and other examinations. I shall take the various branches of the subjects in order, beginning with the most elementary.

The character of a good deal of the teaching of Arithmetic is affected by causes arising from the practical nature of the subject. The master has to keep in view two aims, which, if not different, are at any rate often separate, and his work is tested and criticized from two different standpoints. He must treat the subject so as to derive from it the best educational training for his pupils, and he must satisfy the demands of those who want ready and correct answers to sums and practical questions. No doubt the power of working sums accurately and quickly is sufficiently valuable for its own sake to be worth the trouble spent in gaining it, but in the little time at his disposal the master is often tempted to limit his efforts to developing this power in his pupils. It is so much easier and quicker to give a boy a 'rule' by which he can work out questions in a more or less mechanical fashion than to go through the more difficult and troublesome process of helping him to understand the principles involved and then to think out the method for himself.

The former course will indeed deprive the subject of a greater part of its educational value, but it is likely to pass undetected. Examiners who frame papers in Arithmetic rarely introduce even a single question depending upon a knowledge of the principles as opposed to the practice of the science, and though parents may find out whether their son is able to add up a column of figures correctly or not, they seldom take the trouble to inquire whether he can give the reasons for the processes he adopts. A great point would be gained if questions on the theory of Arithmetic found their way into all Arithmetic papers, and if the difference between good and bad teaching necessarily involved a corresponding difference in 'results.' For it is especially important that in this, the first branch of Mathematics to which a boy is introduced, he should early form the habit of thoroughness, and be compelled, not to learn a set of 'rules,' but to use his intelligence to understand the principles on which they are based. Otherwise it is likely he will never completely recover from the deadening effect which the evasion of all difficulties will have on his mind.

A great deal of what has been said with regard to Arithmetic is true, *mutatis mutandis*, of Algebra. Here also attention should be directed to the principles involved, and not exclusively to the processes by which they are applied. · Without this precaution the study of Algebra is as liable as that of Arithmetic to degenerate into a mechanical exercise. A boy may work through endless numbers of equations and yet have a very hazy idea of the real nature of the steps in the work. He may be able to write down

$$ax + b = c,$$
$$\therefore ax = c - b,$$

and be quite unable to say why the 'sign of b is changed' when the term is 'removed from one side to the other' of the equation.

In solving problems leading to algebraic equations a boy is also apt to regard the expression of the problem in algebraic language as a matter of no moment. He often begins with an inexact or incomplete statement such as 'Let x equal A's share,' or even writes down an equation without any preliminary explanation at all.

An effort to guard against this has led to the introduction of a very useful and valuable feature into some of the modern text-books in the form of a chapter on 'Symbolical Expression.' Here the beginner has to concentrate his attention on the expression in symbols of simple statements, without the distraction furnished by the appearance and solution of an equation.

Clearness and accuracy of thought and language, neatness of arrangement and of work, if always insisted on, are not the least of the benefits which should be derived from the study of Algebra, and indeed they are essential to progress in the subject itself. A boy who has not acquired a neat and orderly style in the earlier stages will be hopelessly at a loss when he attempts the longer or more involved pieces of analysis, depending perhaps on considerations of symmetry, which he is sure to meet with later.

Some of the best, however, of the modern text-books, in their attempt to give greater clearness to their treatment of the subject, seem to introduce a defect of another kind by the excessive subdivision of the chapters. A typical method or example is given and followed by a set of questions of a pre-cisely similar character, then there is another typical example followed by other similar questions, and so on, the whole not being always completed by a set of examples of a more miscellaneous character in which the ingenuity of the boy has to be brought into play to discover the method to be adopted. He may thus know what he will have to do with any question in a particular set even before he reads it, and yet when confronted with one not so labelled, will probably be quite at a loss. When the class is a small one, or when all are working together, the master can overcome the difficulty by dictating a number of general examples of the kind suggested above. This, however, is not easy to do in the case of a large class or of one containing several divisions working at once at different parts of the subject.

In spite of the various attempts to remodel the teaching of Geometry in this country, 'Euclid' is likely to remain for some time to come in England the standard text-book for school purposes. Its merits and defects have been often debated, and this is not the place to revive the controversy. It will be sufficient to indicate the possible danger of a loss of valuable training, were Euclid's Elements replaced by a more arbitrary or less connected series of propositions.

The book, however, is not one into which beginners may be plunged without some previous training, or at any rate some acquaintance with ordinary geometrical figures. Without such an introduction a boy, having mastered a few of the processes of Arithmetic and perhaps of Algebra, finds himself not only confronted by a whole series of unfamiliar terms and ideas, but also expected for the first time to follow out a regular train of reasoning. In addition he is hampered by the poverty of his vocabulary. Of the force of the conjunctions he has absolutely no idea, and he uses 'and,' 'but,' and 'therefore' quite indiscriminately. He begins by learning a set of definitions probably unintelligible to him, or at any rate conveying no definite idea to his mind, followed by a series of 'postulates' and 'axioms' which seem to him meaningless or unnecessary, and he acquires that distaste for Euclid which, except in the case of the brightest boys, seems to be the inevitable result.

Some preliminary acquaintance with geometrical ideas may be given by a few exercises involving merely the drawing with rules and compasses of circles and other simple figures in various positions, and this may be made to lead naturally up to the more formal method of treatment. In this way most of the difficulties arising from the unfamiliarity of the subject disappear. This plan is already often followed in this country, but it is specially interesting in this connexion to notice the scheme of geometrical work as arranged for the four lower classes of the Berlin *Realschulen.* The scheme is taken from the volume of Special Reports[1] published by the Education Department. It is as follows. Of the four classes the Sixth (Sexta) is the lowest.

ELEMENTARY GEOMETRY.

Class VI (one hour a week)—

The simplest constructions with compasses and ruler. Development of simplest geometrical notions through observation, starting from the die. Measuring and drawing of a straight line; measurement of length. Drawing of surface measurements; measurement of

---

[1] *Special Reports on Educational Subjects,* 1896-7, pp. 425-430.

fixed surfaces. Cubic measures and connexion of size and weight. Angle. Construction of a simple triangle.

Class V (two hours a week)—
Revision of the work of Class VI. Further practice with compasses and ruler. Development of geometrical ideas from observation and movement. Fundamental problems. Lines in and at the circle (chords, secants, tangents). Tetrahedron, pyramid, sphere. Written work every fortnight.

Class IV. (three hours a week)—
Mehler: the chief propositions of Elementary Mathematics. The properties of lines, angles, rectilineal figures, and the circle. Simple geometrical construction (analysis, construction, proof). Written work every fortnight.

Class III (three hours a week)—
Mehler: Elementary Mathematics. Equality of rectilineal figures. Proportionality of straight lines. Similar figures. Comparison and measurement of rectilineal figures. Measurement of the circumference and area of a circle. Every fortnight a simple problem (analysis, construction, proof).

In the *Lehrplan* from which this interesting and carefully arranged course is taken one fact in particular may be noted. Whereas in English schools both Arithmetic and Algebra generally precede Euclid in order of study, in the Prussian scheme an effort is made to bring out the parallelism of the geometrical and analytical subjects by the arrangement of the time-table. Elementary Geometry and Arithmetic are begun together in Sexta, and are carried forward in Quinta and Quarta, while it is not until Tertia is reached that Algebra is introduced.

Such a system will have many advantages, but anything of the kind is quite impossible in this country until the necessity of some introduction to Euclid is realized. For as the difficulties of the book lie to a large extent in the earlier portions, it is quite unfitted for a position in the plan such as would naturally be assigned to it.

For while admitting the value of Euclid as an educational instrument, we cannot blind ourselves to some of its drawbacks. The stereotyped series of cut-and-dried propositions often fosters the idea that no other properties of triangles and circles need be considered, or at any rate remembered, and renders less evident the connexion of Geometry with cognate subjects. We must counteract these tendencies by a continual accompaniment of riders and deductions, which are useful not only as furnishing the sole test of sound work and progress, but also as affording opportunities for illustrating the connexion just spoken of. Additional interest will be given to the work by supplementing the course with some of the methods and results of modern projective Geometry.

To derive the fullest possible advantage from the teaching of Mathematics it is necessary that the classes taught should not be too large. There is a tendency to think that mathematical classes may be of almost any size, and if only mechanical accuracy and the ability to work ordinary questions on the various rules be aimed at, no doubt it is possible to do much even with large numbers; but real and effective teaching of such a character as to stimulate the dull boys to try to think for themselves is impossible with more than from twenty-five to thirty in a class. With more than the twenty-five boys individual attention becomes difficult; when the numbers are largely increased it becomes impossible. The dull boys have then a much greater chance of eluding observation and of remaining undisturbed in their indifference than in a class sufficiently small to allow of the master discovering the extent to which his explanations have been understood. And these are just the boys who would profit most by being compelled to exercise their minds on the matters considered.

The position of a subject in the school curriculum and the amount of time devoted to it depend upon the value of that subject as a means of education, using the word in its broadest sense. Mathematics is mainly responsible for the development of the logical faculty and the power of abstract reasoning, but it leaves untouched equally important sides of a boy's character and intellect. Literary taste, imagination, and the power of observation require also to be cultivated, and for these it offers little or no opportunity. Without entering upon a discussion of the relative value of various subjects from this point of view, it will be enough for our purpose to point out that the general opinion in this country, as gathered from a comparison of various school time-tables, seems to assign about five hours a week, or one-fifth of the whole available time, as a proper proportion to be given to Mathematics. This opinion seems to be confirmed by experience in Germany, if we may judge from the time-tables given in the article on the Berlin *Realschulen* from which I have already quoted. It is amusing, however, to notice how different a view was formerly taken. We find for instance from old records that early in the present century at the Manchester Grammar School 'Tuesday, Thursday and Saturday were half-holidays and devoted to the study of Mathematics.'

In most subjects the average boy reaches a certain limit beyond which it seems impossible for him to make any substantial advance. In Mathematics this is specially noticeable. Many who have made a certain amount of progress in Algebra and Euclid may seem quite incapable of getting any real grasp of Trigonometry. I have known a boy do fairly well to this point and fail completely at Analytical Geometry. It follows that the amount of work done in the ordinary school routine is not likely to be much extended, and that the number of those who go beyond this will still be limited. The master therefore who has to do with those reading higher work, instead of having to teach boys of all degrees of ability, probably in classes of considerable size, will be concerned with a much smaller number, all of whom will have some natural aptitude for Mathematics and some interest in it. His task is on the whole an easier one ; he has only to direct and help, and is not called upon to supply the motive power.

The order in which the various subjects are to be taken up is open to much discussion, and it is neither wise nor even possible to lay down or follow any hard and fast line. In spite of the advantage arising from the sense of progress that a boy has when he reaches a new subject in his reading, it seems best in practice to demand of him a fairly thorough knowledge of Algebra and Trigonometry before proceeding further. I do not mean to imply that he should on his first reading be able to work out practically any question that he is likely to meet with in these subjects, but that he should at any rate have gone carefully over the greater portion of the ground. At the same time he will have extended his knowledge of Pure Geometry so that it will include some of the more modern methods and results, and he will then be in a position to proceed without loss of time to Analytical Geometry and the branches of Mechanics. Much trouble is saved later if a boy begins by becoming fairly expert in the use of what are really his tools.

The question is largely one of time. We are surrounded by an ever-increasing number of examinations from which it is impossible to escape, and the problem to be solved is how to prepare for these without sacrificing thoroughness and genuine work to a mere scramble for prizes. The various examinations, such as those for mathematical entrance scholarships at the older Universities, have been so extended in range and increased in difficulty, and the competition has now become so keen, that preparation for them is no longer a mere matter of two or three terms. When a boy has covered the ground required, he has to set himself to gain the power not only of solving the problems set, but of doing so in a very short time. This is only possible after a very considerable amount of practice, and necessitates, except for the most brilliant boys, earlier specialization than was formerly the case or than is even now desirable. And my own experience has shown that even the best boy mathematicians may require time for the acquisition of this kind of facility, and that an extra year's work may do wonders in its development. Regular weekly miscellaneous problem papers, either taken from some of the published collections or, better still, arranged by the master himself to suit his own circumstances, are a great help, but in some form or other the practice must be ensured.

The arrangement by which a number of colleges are grouped together for examination purposes, though it no doubt discourages 'pot-hunting,' sometimes presses rather hardly on the poorer candidates, as if from any cause they are prevented from doing themselves justice at any particular time, they may find themselves altogether at a loss. It also tends to encourage earlier specialization, since with fewer opportunities of retrieving a piece of ill fortune, even a really clever boy, whose abilities are amply sufficient to warrant his going to a University, yet may find that his parents cannot afford to send him there unaided, and will therefore be anxious to run no risks when he competes.

Scholarships are won by the power of solving problems, not by the thorough and intelligent study of book-work, which is certainly of not less importance, though it lacks the encouragement of high marks. For instance, the ability to sum given infinite series is more 'useful' than a clear idea as to the conditions under which the summations are possible. On the other hand, the questions are generally framed so as to demand a very thorough knowledge of the points involved and to discourage a merely superficial acquaintance.

The real danger is lest, amid the multitude of examinations, from which hardly any one altogether escapes, the study of Mathematics, instead of being followed for its own sake, should merely be valued for its pecuniary rewards. It is here that the influence of the master may make itself felt. Success will attend him in following the higher aims in proportion to his own enthusiasm for the subject and to his possession of that power of personal contact with others which enables him to inspire them with the same feeling.

H. L. JOSELAND.

THE TEACHING OF NATURAL SCIENCE

It is only within the last fifty years that the material progress due to scientific discovery and the increase of international competition have raised up a strong opposition to the pre-eminence of Latin and Greek as the sole instruments of education in our public schools. In the early stages of the movement an attack was made on the older schools, where the teaching of science was indeed eventually introduced, but reluctantly and in a very subordinate position. This perhaps premature attempt was, as might have been expected, a complete failure as regards results, and to this extent has operated prejudicially, that it has given a show of reason to the reiterated assertions of the inherent inadaptability of science as an instrument of education, and has encouraged the numerous local grammar schools to persevere in their opposition to the change. But the demands of the industrial classes in the large and growing centres of manufacture and commerce have given rise more recently to special technical schools, which are rapidly being converted into secondary schools on the basis of science, and are displacing the endowed schools.   These new schools are however organized on utilitarian principles, and it is a misfortune that science should have established itself as a subject of instruction in schools of a technical type, before taking up its proper place, on its own merits as an educational subject, in schools of an 'Hellenic' type.

For the unique position claimed for Latin, 'that it is the only subject which should run through all education from the infant school to the University,' is based upon the assumption that there must be one path for all, and that all are endowed with an aptitude and taste for the same subject. But any master of a form on a classical side which has not yet been weeded out by turning over the weaklings to the modern side will readily admit variation in individual tendencies.   It will be admitted further that it is of the greatest importance in education to give attention to varying dispositions, and to direct the education of a boy along the line of his own mental inclination and ability. If this be so, then it can be safely asserted that there is no single subject which can possibly form the principal educational agent for all pupils. Although during the early period of a boy's life many subjects will be viewed by him with equal indifference, there soon comes a time when the individual taste is more pronounced, while yet he recognizes that some one subject—for which he may or may not have either taste or capacity—is regarded by the school authorities as more important than others. His position in the school and his position in his class are an expression of the opinion held concerning him, and continually represent to him his own powers and possibilities; but they are decided by the subject which is regarded as best and highest, and is consequently the determining factor in his school work. If the subject is not one suited to his capacities, this may have a depressing and deadening effect upon him. It will not however be necessary that it should be entirely given up, but it is necessary on the other hand that it should not always take the position in which it represents the highest excellence, and that it should be possible for the boy to have some other subject more suited to his taste and mental bent placed before him, by which his position in form and in school may be gauged, and which will enable him to estimate his own possibilities at a higher and truer value. If this is done, the gain to the boy in self-respect and self-confidence is such that he will benefit more than formerly by continuing, as a subsidiary subject, the subject which has been dethroned, and will make greater progress in it. On the highest grounds, a school which puts before itself 'the educating not for this or that special function, but simply for manhood,' must seek to interest and occupy the learner's mind, and must devise curricula accordingly. This argument was clearly understood and admitted by the Italian school-masters of the early Renaissance. This is so

interesting that I will quote at length a passage
which represents the views held by Vittorino da
Feltre: 'In truth, we are not to expect that every
boy will display the same tastes or the same degree
of mental capacity; and whatever our own predi-
lection may be, we recognize that we must follow
Nature's lead.   Now she has endowed no one with
aptitude for all kinds of knowledge; very few indeed
have talent in three or four directions, but every one
has received some gift, if only we can discover it.'
The writer goes on to compare the human intellect
to the soil, with its varying degree of fertility, here
good, here poor, but even the worst capable of some
response to suitable cultivation.   'Hence,' says his
biographer, 'he sought out that subject and that
method of instruction which he believed to be best
adapted to each individual intelligence.   Upon the
dullest he would bestow infinite pains, that by devising simple tasks or some special form of training
he might meet the needs even of the least promising
scholars.'   'We may not count,' he would say,
'upon capacity for Letters in every child; and
Literature, though the best, is not the only educational instrument.   The end to be kept in view must
be to interest and occupy the learner's mind and to
devise a curriculum accordingly.'

From this reasoning it follows that it should be
possible for a boy to be educated through the agency
of the subject for which he has most inclination and
ability; not that he should give up all but this

subject—for it will generally, if not always, be better to learn three or four subjects—but that this should be his main subject, by which he will be chiefly judged; and the object of schoolmasters is to bring as many subjects as possible into that organized condition which adapts them as instruments of education for schools. Now whatever the state of science may have been when the attempt was first made to introduce it into schools, it is now claimed that it is so systematized as to form a subject adapted to take its place side by side with classics. No doubt there are many classical scholars and classical schoolmasters who hold that 'the taste for, and proficiency in, classics indicates with certainty the possession of a higher type of intelligence,' but this is not much help to them in dealing with the different types of boys met with in every public school; and, instead of dwelling on this, I will endeavour to show the lines along which science should be taught if it is to be worthy of a place in schools, what place it should hold in the school curricula, and for what kind of assistance schoolmasters may look to the Universities and other outside bodies which control the work of schools.

What I have already said is practically an argument in favour of the system of parallel Classical and Modern Sides, on which respectively Classics and Science are the main subjects, and other subjects subsidiary. It is freely said that Modern Sides are the refuges of the idle, that some boys rapidly discover an inaptitude for anything that is hard, and that the principle of working along the line of least resistance is highly appreciated by them. There is a certain amount of truth in this. The difficulty is, however, easily met by the schoolmaster when the Modern Sides are well organized, and the remedy is entirely in their hands and in those of the Univer-sities. Let the Sides of the school be recognized as distinctly parallel. Let it be possible for a boy on a Modern Side to reach the highest position in the school and aspire to its highest rewards, and let the Universities adjust their examinations to admit boys from a Modern Side without their having to turn aside from their regular work and 'cram' some special subject; then the standard and position of these Sides would be improved, and the distinction between the 'Classical' and 'Modern'—which is altogether an unreal one—would disappear.

But before going further, an objection may be noticed that comes from a quarter whence we would perhaps least expect it. It is urged by some dis-tinguished professors of medicine that in their experience students coming to biological studies direct from the classics do better than those who have had instruction in science. If this were true, it would not seriously affect the position we have taken up in pleading for science in the cause of education, but it is a serious attack on utilitarian grounds. But is it true? We very much doubt it. Surely these professors drew their conclusions from impressions made by two sets of students whose relative rate of progress is contrary to expectation. It is, in the professors' idea, equally contrary to expectation that a classical boy should do well in biological studies, and that a boy who has worked at science should do badly. The fact is that the comparison is made between a capable boy who, because of his abilities, has been kept at Classics, and a boy of much less ability who, because of this, has been turned over to Science. Let the professors compare a capable boy who has been well trained in scientific method with a boy of small ability who has been kept at Classics. The long list of able students of Science who have had a sound training is left unnoticed; they do not strike the attention by their incongruity. Moreover, in judging of the value of scientific training, critics must be careful to distinguish between a knowledge of the facts of Science gained by listening to lectures, and the results obtained by a training in scientific method. It is for the latter and not the former that we plead.

What place then should Science take in public and secondary schools? There will be no difficulty in answering this question if we accept as a fundamental principle that education should proceed by guiding the natural tendencies of children. It will be clear that the methods of the Kindergarten should be continued in the preparatory school, and adapted— as Froebel intended to adapt them—to a later stage than the childhood of the nursery. This means that in every preparatory school Science should form a part of the general education—and by Science is meant not simply object lessons or lectures (valuable as they are in exciting interest and imparting knowledge), but the encouragement of observation and thought by making full use of the inquisitiveness of a boy's nature, his natural desire to handle *things* and to experiment with them. In other words, the Science teaching must be experimental. Now as all children are eager to give expression to their ideas of the shape and colour of objects by drawing and painting, this eagerness must be encouraged, and the faculty directed by lessons in memory-drawing, in drawing from objects, and at a later stage in copying from the flat. Such lessons should be continued in the preparatory school, and when the observing and inventive faculties have been exercised, then the boy should be introduced to empirical Geometry. Practical Geometry should be taught in all preparatory schools. Young boys should be able to use the simple mathematical instruments, viz. the dividers, compasses, protractors, scales, and set-squares, learn to bisect lines and angles, draw perpendiculars and parallels, construct angles, triangles, squares, parallelograms, and tangents to circles, and know the chief properties of the elementary geometrical figures. It is best in beginning this Geometry to use tracing paper only. By that means lines and angles can be bisected, perpendiculars and parallels drawn, and triangles and squares constructed. Much can be done by the methods of trial and failure, by cutting out and superposition—methods which not only appeal to the juvenile mind, but give familiarity with geometrical figures, and incidentally teach many of the principles of formal Geometry. From this Geometry the pupil will pass to Mensuration. And here, if Mensuration is to be of any educational value, it must not be the Mensuration of the text-book. No formulae must be known or seen. The area of a square must be found by dividing it into unit squares or fractions of the unit, and the areas of oblongs must be found by similar methods. All other figures must be reduced to their equivalent oblong, and in solid mensuration all volumes must be reduced to their equivalent prisms. The balance, drawing paper, and squared paper must be brought into use, that the relations between the areas and volumes and their linear dimensions may be discovered. Cubes, prisms, cones, cylinders, pyramids should be made out of cardboard, and their surface areas and volumes found. The dimensions of suitable solid objects of regular shape should be obtained by actual measurement. The mere arithmetical calculation of areas and volumes is of very little educational value. To find the area of a trapezoid by following some rule is worse than useless; what is wanted is, by cutting out paper to show to what oblong it is equal in area, and then by dividing the oblong into squares to find its area. It is by systematically proving and verifying that scientific conceptions are formed. The next step will be to lead the pupil to the relation between mass and volume, i.e. to density. Small boys can be given cubes of equal size, and be set to weigh them, and compare the densities of different substances. They can then be given cubes or prisms of unequal sizes, and be set to find their volumes and densities. From solids the class can be taken to liquids, and hence to bodies of irregular shape. This is all work which appeals to the interest of boys between the ages of ten and thirteen; it awakens their intelligence and prepares the way for scientific conceptions, and what is perhaps of equal practical importance, it is work which can quite well be taught by a mathematical master who is in sympathy with the methods, and is therefore work which can readily and systematically be adopted by preparatory schools.

Space will not allow me to attempt in detail a scheme of Science teaching for public schools, but an outline of the principles which must be our guide in forming such a scheme will be useful, and an agreement as to this must be reached if Science is to be established satisfactorily as part of our educational machinery. I can best illustrate these principles, and at the same time keep within my personal experience, if I confine myself to the science of Physics, or to the sciences which are correlated under the name of Physics. The first principle of importance is that these sciences must be taken in their natural scientific order. This simple truth, which conforms with all the theory and practice of education, is so far from being generally recognized that it is ignored by all—or nearly all—the examining bodies. In their syllabuses we find mechanics, heat, light, sound, and electricity put down as alternative subjects, and the examiners doing their best to set questions on each subject which may be answered in some kind of way without any knowledge of the others [1]. Now if we divide boys' time at school from the age of thirteen into two parts—from thirteen to fifteen, and from fifteen to eighteen (the ages being average ages of the classes), then the work of this first period should be confined to Practical Geometry and Mensuration, Hydrostatics, Statics, and Heat, leaving Graphic Geometry, Dynamics, Optics, Electricity, and more advanced 'Heat' for the second: Geometry, Mensuration, Hydrostatics, and Statics are usually treated mathematically, and therefore do not suggest themselves as suitable educational subjects for boys below the age of fifteen—i. e. for boys

[1] This unscientific way of teaching and examining in Science is illustrated every day by notices of County Council grants in aid of Science to Secondary Schools. Only recently I read a letter in the local press asking for subscriptions for the teaching of Electricity. It appeared that the County Council had granted a sum of money for electrical apparatus, and if £30 could be added to this grant it would be possible to add Electricity as a subject to the school course. No fault can be found with the school authorities. No doubt it is easier in this experimental stage to get public money for Electricity than it is for Hydrostatics. In fact, Electricity is a good word to conjure with.

in the Fourth Forms of a school—whose knowledge
of Mathematics is confined to rudimentary Arithmetic,
Euclid, and Algebra. But this kind of teaching is
not what is meant. The teaching must be based
upon graphic methods and upon a few well-defined
experiments, requiring little apparatus, and this of a
simple character. Geometry studied by the method
described above will lead to a practical knowledge
of Trigonometry, will illustrate Algebra, and perhaps
add interest to Mathematics as a whole by solving
equations and showing their genesis. This may
be said to be beyond boys of the age, but the
great virtue of the graphic and experimental methods
is that they fix the attention for a sufficiently long
time for the principles involved to 'soak in.' The
experiments must be carefully graded, so as to
separate the difficulties and introduce new ideas
one by one, slowly and with precision. Science
teaching has often failed by succumbing to the
'lecture room' temptation of communicating a large
number of facts, but doing no more than exercise
the memory and appeal to the interest of the hearers.
This is not teaching scientific method. But unfortunately so unorganized at present is our system
that this method is somewhat naturally regarded
as the proper basis of examination, and thus the
mischief is perpetuated. Teachers look to the
examinations to see what they are to teach, and
examiners look to the schools to see what is taught.

The fact is that the time is now ripe for a radical

change to be made in all Science examinations in the direction of delimitation. What has often been said as to English teaching in schools can be well applied to the teaching of Science. From the large number of facts we must select a few upon which to exer-cise the mind of the boy. If the soaking process is a right one, we must pick out a few experiments and devote ourselves to them. 'The honey bee visits but a few flowers ; the butterfly ranges at will, and brings nothing home.' Instead of the medley of facts and theories at present taught, a boy should be given a simple set of apparatus and be led to study a few principles or laws, varying the conditions as many ways as may lead to the laws becoming clear to him. Suppose, for instance, the subject is Statics, and two hours per week are given to it ; then one term would be devoted to studying the 'composition of forces,' one to 'parallel forces,' and one to machines. The apparatus required for the first term would be the now well-known 'pulley-board,' with sets of weights, and, as variations, models of cranes, struts, roof-trusses, and simple bridge-girders—all depending upon a few simple principles. The structures would be measured and carefully drawn to scale, and the geometrical dia-gram representing the forces acting along each member of the structure would be drawn to a force-scale ; only where the mathematical skill existed need any attempt be made to use Mathematics. Indeed one of the disadvantages of allowing Mathematies to be used at this stage is that the 'Science' is soon forgotten in the solving of problems and getting of results. For the second term levers and weights and spring balances will be required, and, as practical illustrations, models of loaded trusses and girders. For the third term pulley tackle, screw jackets, differential wheels and axles, winches, and other machines actually used in trades will be required. The class will first study the geometrical properties of each machine, its velocity or displacement ratio, and will then proceed to investigate the forces required for a number of loads, and work out the mechanical advantage, efficiency and force absorbed in overcoming the friction of each machine. As far as possible, and according to the capabilities of the class, all the results will be represented graphically. Each subject can be treated in the same way, by choosing a few leading principles, and devising simple experiments so as to lead the class step by step to discover, as it were, the principles for themselves.

A word or two as to these experiments. They must be always *direct*, not experiments involving complication in the quantity to be measured. The ideas themselves are difficult enough for the beginner. It is some time before the young boy grasps the meaning of density, or is capable of separating mass, volume, and area from each other. We must therefore design experiments which do not call up any difficulties but the one under study. If the meaning of density is the object placed before the class, then the substances must at first be given in the form of cubes or prisms, so that the difficulty of volume is made as small as possible; later on cylinders or even spheres may be used, and finally irregular solids. Or to take an illustration from a later stage, in Ohm's Law. The first object is to understand the meaning of Ohm's Law, not simply to be able to write down and use its mathematical expression. The class will therefore be set to find the electromotive force by the heat generated in a given wire when a measured number of Coulombs passes through it. The quantity of heat will be measured and expressed in Joules, the current passing will be measured in Ampères, and the Joules per Coulomb or Volts determined. The ratio of the Volts to the Ampères will be found for different currents. The point I wish to make clear is that each quantity should as far as possible be measured directly and expressed in well-understood units, and the relation between the quantities or the laws of Physics determined. This too is the historical order of discovery, and for a teacher no works are so suggestive as those of the earliest investigators—Cavendish, Black, Faraday, and Joule.

A word of warning may not be out of place here. Practical work as the basis of Science teaching has now found such powerful support, being endowed by County Councils and the Science and Art Department, that there is a danger of the handicraft methods of the technical schools of London and other great centres being followed in secondary schools to the exclusion of purely scientific methods. The school-master has always to bear in mind that his subject is to be made an instrument of education, and that processes which may appear best towards attaining knowledge are not necessarily the best for the purpose of imparting method.

My object has been to show what place is claimed for Science in the curriculum of a school, and to indicate the lines on which the teaching of it may best run, and in doing so I have had constantly in view the technical difficulties which beset a subject, if it is to be added to the number of the recognized instruments of education. To take the place of a suitable 'form subject,' it must be one in which the boys themselves work, not one in which all the work is done by the master; it must be one in which lessons may be set regularly, with a reasonable hope on the part of the master of being able to exact them. There is more difficulty in this respect with Science than with Latin or Mathematics, yet we may say that the difficulty is now overcome. The position of Science to-day is not what it was ten years ago, and schoolmasters who may have some doubts on this important point may be asked to believe that Science teaching is now something different from 'listening to a lecture, taking notes, and copying them out.' That this is so is due to the influence of technical education, the influence, that is, of teachers of Science drawn from other quarters than from the Universities, who have brought a fresh breeze of the workshop into a somewhat academic atmosphere, and to the sympathetic manner in which the Universities—especially the University of Cambridge—have infused into Science teaching their own philosophic spirit. The examinations should now take a step forward, and adjust themselves to a new order of things. The Oxford and Cambridge Joint Board and the Local Examinations considerably influence the teaching in the secondary schools, and directly or indirectly that of all public schools; and if, as we believe, their influence should first be brought to bear upon the elementary teaching, the examination syllabuses for boys of fifteen or sixteen years must be so modified as to reduce the number of subjects, to define and limit each subject, and to insist—if possible by actual practical examination—on experimental methods of teaching. Both the Joint Board and the Local Syndicates are moving tentatively in this direction, and the schools look to them to accelerate the requisite changes. The highest standard will be that of the College scholarship examinations, and a comparison of the papers set by the Cambridge Colleges will show that those responsible for these examinations are anxious to see the subjects limited in extent and taught in scientific sequence, and by direct experimental methods[1].

[1] This cannot be said of Oxford, where Physics is encouraged neither by the scholarship examinations nor by

But the whole question of Science scholarships is, from a wider point of view, a difficult one. It has been said—and it is no doubt true—that scholarships in Science are awarded to candidates who know no Latin, and cannot spell English. What is the cause of this, and how is it to be remedied? It is obviously out of the power of the Universities to prevent it, as they already exact an entrance examination in Latin, Greek, English, and Mathematics, though with the result that the first two are crammed, without leaving much permanent result. It would seem that both the fault and the remedy lie with the schools. Science is not taught throughout the schools, and hence when at a certain age (nearly seventeen) the discovery is made that a boy will not gain a scholarship in Classics, when in fact his classical master considers that he would now be better for a change of subject, he is transferred to Science; and, need pressing, he must give up all his time to it, and forget the small amount of Latin and Greek he has learnt. If Science had formed a part of his regular school-work, he would have gained a fairly sound knowledge of the elements, and when the change took place, it would not be necessary

the University teaching. The scholarship papers are still a mixture of easy mathematical mechanics and questions in such advanced subjects as double refraction and polarization, without much regard apparently to what can reasonably be done in schools; and the highest honours in the Schools are practically unattainable by any one but a skilled mathematician.

to specialize so completely. With this preliminary training up to the age of sixteen a boy could reasonably expect to prepare for a scholarship in Classics, Mathematics, Science or Modern Languages, and at the same time to give the necessary hours to his other subjects.

F. W. SANDERSON.

'It is undoubtedly in the highest degree desirable that all great advances in Science should become the common property of all cultivated men. And this can only be done by introducing into the course of a liberal education such studies as unfold and fix in men's minds the fundamental ideas upon which the new discovered truths rest. . . . By the discoveries which are made and by the clearness and evidence which, after a time, the truths thus discovered acquire, one portion of knowledge after another becomes elementary, and if we would really secure this progress and make men share in it, these new portions must be treated as elementary in the constitution of a liberal education.'— WHEWELL, *The Philosophy of the Inductive Sciences*, book xiii. ch. 3.

THE sentences quoted above form part of a plea for the more general recognition of the Natural Sciences as an instrument of education. They were written more than fifty years ago; yet, in spite of the great authority which Dr. Whewell possessed, so little has been done to give effect to his recommendations, that it is even now an almost impossible task to write on the relations subsisting between the teaching of Natural Science in public schools and the study of Natural Science in the Universities. Impossible, because the relations are of so slender a kind that, for all practical purposes, they are non-existent. The Universities do not require any knowledge of Natural Science from those who join them, and the majority of the classical public schools make no attempt to supply what is not required. Hence, instead of describing an existing order of things, one is obliged to expose disorder and advocate sweeping measures of reform.

The attitude of Oxford and Cambridge towards Natural Science is peculiar, and though it differs somewhat in the two Universities it is in its most important features the same. The Natural Sciences have long been recognized as subjects of higher education by both Universities. At Cambridge there is the Natural Science Tripos, at Oxford the Honour School of Natural Science, as an avenue to the Arts degree, and both Oxford and Cambridge, but especially the latter, have spent very large sums of money in providing all that is necessary in the way of museums, laboratories, apparatus and lectures. But whilst recognizing and even encouraging Natural Science as an academic study, neither University has shown any indication of recognizing the Natural Sciences as an indispensable element in a liberal education. A man may go up to either Cambridge or Oxford, pass all his examinations, and attain to the highest honours that the University can bestow upon him, without having so much as a rudimentary comprehension of the Natural Sciences. To this extent both Universities alike are indifferent to the subject, and their indifference infects the classical public schools. The consequence is that the great advances in Science are so far from being the common property of all cultivated men, that those who are styled cultivated are ignorant of the Sciences, whilst many of those who know the Sciences are held not to be cultivated.

It will be the object of this essay to show that a man who is ignorant of Science is no more entitled to be called cultivated, at the end of the nineteenth century, than a man who is ignorant of the Classics ; that every subject which should form a part of a liberal education must be taught, and thoroughly taught, at the public schools, or it will run the risk of not being taught at all ; and finally that it rests with the Universities to decide what are the elements of a liberal education, and so to arrange their entrance examinations that the schools should be forced to abide by their decision.

But first of all we must consider further the present position of Natural Science in public schools. And let it be understood here that, wherever reference is made to 'schools,' those schools are meant which profess to give a liberal education, without reference to the necessities of any technical, professional, or commercial career. These schools set the standard of a liberal education, and the multiplication of them is as effective in confirming the defects as in spreading the advantages of the system which they encourage.

There is some provision for the teaching of Natural

Science in all, or very nearly all, these schools. In most it is an optional subject, undertaken by a few boys who show special aptitude for it, or by those who are set to the study of Science in the hope that they may make some compensation for their failure in other branches of learning. In some few schools Science is compulsory, but creditable as the intention may be, the results are not encouraging. Those results must be tested, firstly by the number and merit of the candidates who enter for the Natural Science scholarships and exhibitions offered by different Colleges at Oxford and Cambridge ; secondly by the scientific attainments of the average boy who does not compete for scholarships and exhibitions.

The number of scholarships is far greater at Cambridge than at Oxford, a circumstance which is chiefly due to the different systems which prevail in the two Universities. At Oxford the age of candidates for scholarships is strictly limited, and therefore it is rarely the case that a man is eligible to compete for a scholarship at the end of his first year's residence at the University. At Cambridge the age limit is wider, and it is not unusual for men to enter for Science scholarships at the end of their first year of residence, and on the results, in part, of their reading at the University. Further, the classical tests are so much more severe at Oxford than at Cambridge, that boys who have had a 'modern' education are driven, by fear of failure in their Classics, to the latter University. Thus it

K

becomes apparent that the results of Science teaching
in public schools is more accurately gauged by the
Oxford than by the Cambridge scholarship examinations. Now, at Oxford the candidates for the Natural
Science scholarships are few in number, and they
seldom attain to a high average standard of merit.
Frequently one or two boys show considerable
ability, but the rest are far below scholarship standard, and it is sometimes the case that a College
is unable to award a scholarship because no candidate of sufficient merit has presented himself.
When one considers the large numbers and general
excellence of the candidates for the much more
numerous classical scholarships, this does not speak
very well for the teaching of Natural Science at
public schools. Though its system is different, the
final experience of Cambridge is the same ; for it
is admitted there that if the Science scholarships
were competed for solely by boys coming from
schools, either it would be necessary to lower the
standards, or it would hardly be possible to award
the full number of scholarships.

But if the chosen and specially prepared candidates
are disappointing, what of the rank and file ? They
are frankly innocent of any knowledge of Science
whatsoever, and their innocence is as great whether
they have had to attend Science classes in a junior
form in a public school, or whether they have not.
As the number of candidates in the Science Tripos
at Cambridge and in the Honour School of Natural

Science at Oxford is far in excess of the number of successful and unsuccessful candidates for scholarships, it follows that a considerable number of men have to learn the whole of their scientific work at the Universities. Starting with no knowledge at all, they have to begin with the very alphabet of their subject, and when they have scarcely learned that, they are hurried on to the advanced studies necessary for obtaining a place in the class list. Their whole University career is devoted to cramming, first the preliminary subjects in which they must pass, secondly the final subjects in which they hope to take honours. The result is unfortunate both to the student and to the teacher. The student is absorbed in acquiring new facts, and has little time for reflection. He comes to regard the scientific subjects in which he has to pass as so many disagreeable tasks, to be learned as quickly as possible, and as quickly forgotten; and he fails to obtain that comprehensive grasp of the elements of all the Sciences which is essential to breadth of view and solidity of judgement. The teacher is in an even worse plight, for he is obliged to force his pupils along the prescribed road, and he cannot stay to explain and develop the principles which are the basis of all the Sciences. He expends an enormous amount of time and energy in driving home rudimentary ideas and facts which might well have been learned in childhood, and has little leisure left for the reading, research and reflection which are necessary in an ever-progressive subject. None but those who have experienced it can realize how much the teacher loses in force and originality by being obliged, term after term and year after year, to push a number of young men at hot haste through the veriest rudiments of the Natural Sciences. It is no doubt due to the weariness produced by this monotonous task that so many men, whose youth was full of promise, fall off in interest and spirit after they have spent a few years in teaching Science at the Universities. At the end of it all, the average Science man acquires a number of facts, and perhaps gets a good degree; but he is hardly a cultivated man, for he has been forced to specialize before he really understood the fundamental parts of his subject, and his ideas are consequently limited. The Science scholar is of course in a better position, for he starts with a tolerably good knowledge of fact, and, if he has been well taught, he has some ideas and plenty of time for general reading and reflection. But he suffers to a great extent because of the others; for lectures and tuition are perforce brought down to the understanding of those who begin in ignorance, and the teachers are too much engrossed in bringing up the rearguard to be able to give sufficient time and thought to those who are in the van. This is one result, then, of the neglect of Science in early youth, that University studies in that subject are chiefly primary studies, when they ought to be advanced and philosophical.

But after all, the Science student does end by knowing a good deal of Science, and he has had some training in Classics and in Ancient and Modern History. He can therefore fairly lay claim to having had a liberal education, and he has learned the invaluable lesson that he must form his own judgements and rely upon experience rather than on books. Can we say as much for those who, having arrived at the Universities ignorant of the Sciences, remain in that ignorance to the end of their days? Is it possible that persons who are strangers to the vast range of ideas and speculations which have sprung from the advance of Natural Science—is it possible that they can be called more cultivated than their scientific colleagues? ' No,' it will be answered, ' but there is scarcely anybody who is so ignorant of Science as you allege. The general principles of the Natural Sciences are so universally acted upon and talked about, and are in their essence so easy of comprehension, that any ordinarily intelligent person is capable of comprehending them without any special preparation.' This is the commonly received but none the less erroneous opinion, and it is of the greatest importance that its error should be recognized; for as long as it prevails, so long will the educational value of the Natural Sciences be underestimated by those who have no experience of them. It must be understood that the study of the Natural Sciences requires a habit of thought which is not easily attainable; and that to apprehend its principles requires serious labour and a forced steadiness of thought, such as is not produced by any other discipline. To those who urge that well-educated persons come to know enough of the Sciences for all practical purposes, one may reply that indications constantly occur in conversation and in literature of the great inaccuracy and vagueness of thought which prevails respecting scientific subjects. If only literary persons, highly educated as they are from one point of view, would recognize that they are quite uneducated from another point of view, that they have neither the clear conceptions nor the habits of thought necessary to the comprehension of the Natural Sciences, and that their attempts to deal with them only raise a smile amongst scientific men, the position for which we are striving would be nearly won.

There are many common errors about the place of Science in education which must be dealt with here, and in dealing with them it is scarcely possible to avoid a comparison between classical and scientific methods. But since we must make the comparison, let us disclaim any intention of underrating the value of classical study. It is freely acknowledged that the Classics are absolutely indispensable to culture; that the study of the dead languages affords a means of training which, for particular purposes, cannot be surpassed; and that there is contained in the writings of the ancients all that is best and highest in many departments of human thought.

All that is asked here is the recognition of the fact that, though the Classics may teach us much, they cannot and do not teach us all. The Greeks attempted but failed to illuminate the Natural Sciences, and their failure is evidence that they had not acquired those special habits of thought which are necessary for the purpose. Clearly, then, we cannot expect to learn the methods of scientific study from the ancients. Yet it is one of the most prevalent errors that a mind disciplined by the grammar of the dead languages, with just a tincture of Mathematics and Geometry, is capable of dealing with all departments of thought.

In a classical education, as it is at present conducted, the chief instrument, and the one held in most esteem, is Grammar. Since it is through grammar that we attain to accuracy and felicity of expression, it must be allowed that the study of it is exceedingly important; but as an exclusive instrument of mental training it is deficient in many important requirements, and, as we shall argue, it actually perverts the understanding. Grammar consists of a set of arbitrary rules not supported by reasoning, and to every grammatical rule there are exceptions of which no explanation is given. A boy's education begins, and often ends, in learning by heart the rules and the exceptions and in applying them in translation. The result of this practice is a mental habit of refusing to reason upon things as they present themselves, instead of judging them by a fixed standard of rules. Supposing that a boy is of an inquisitive turn of mind and asks the reason for the rules which he has learned; he is told that caprice is the determining factor, for if the rules of grammar are not capricious, the exceptions certainly are. As he proceeds from grammar to the study of idiom, to poetry and imaginative writing, and finally to human history and politics, he becomes more and more convinced of the power of this caprice in the conduct of affairs. All the while he remains ignorant, or, if not ignorant, unconvinced of the fundamental thought of Science, the conviction of the existence of a universal bond of law. It is true that he is taught some Mathematics and Geometry, and these subjects are supposed to supplement the deficiencies of his classical training. They might be admirably adapted to the purpose, but like Grammar they are taught by rule and by rote, and so they are made valueless. If proof be required of the futility of Mathematics and Geometry, as they are commonly taught in classical schools, it is to be found in the utter inability of the average student to solve the simplest problems arising out of the two first books of Euclid.

Our argument has been that exclusively classical study, imperfectly backed as it is by Arithmetic and Geometry, though it may teach the application of fixed rules to special cases, is destructive of the habit of inquiry and reasoning. The argument will be distasteful to many, but there is much evidence to support it. Take for example the average public schoolboy who begins the study of Science at the Universities. Brought up, as he has been, on book-work, and accustomed to learn things by heart, he finds the greatest difficulty in making an observation or an experiment, and it is quite beyond his powers to draw conclusions from its results. He is ready enough to learn facts from books and to repeat rules laid down by his teachers, but it is long before he can accustom himself to reason steadily and clearly on the subjects laid before him. 'Forced steadiness of thought,' a habit of mind justly extolled by Whewell, is the last thing which is to be expected from the product of a classical public school.

The apologists for a classical education do in fact admit that a public school education is not adapted to develop the reasoning powers. For they argue that young minds are receptive but not reasonable ; that boys learn easily by heart and retain what they have learnt, coming to see its reason afterwards when their minds are matured. They justify their methods by saying that experience has shown that the memory may be cultivated when young, and that in later years, whilst the reasoning powers are developed, memory becomes proportionally weaker.

The argument is plausible because it is partly true, and in so far as it is true, one may well ask why the great principles and the more important facts of Science should not as well be committed to memory as the genders of Latin nouns ? But it is only partly true. The memory is stronger in youth than in more mature age, but it is not the case that the reasoning powers cannot be called forth in youth, or that, if they are called forth, they prejudice the memory. The apologists forget that beside the experience of classical teaching there is growing up an experience of scientific teaching, and that this newer experience stands in direct contradiction to the old. There is no reputable teacher of Science who would not assert that the attempt to teach Science through the memory alone is highly prejudicial. Nothing is more clearly proved than the fact that boys, if they are properly taught, are capable of apprehending and reasoning upon the elementary truths of Science, and that their progress is directly proportional to the exercise of their reasoning faculties, and inversely proportional to the exercise of their memories.

Young boys are almost universally inquisitive about natural phenomena; and they give practical expression of their inquisitiveness by collecting all sorts of natural subjects and by making rudimentary attempts at experiments. Experience has shown that this inquisitiveness, if rightly directed, may be made to lead to a very sound though quite elementary knowledge of Natural Science; and further that the principles thus learned in early youth are retained with peculiar freshness and distinctness in after years, and afford a very secure foundation for further knowledge. Unfortunately this foundation is very seldom laid. The natural curiosity of the boy is generally checked because it is tiresome; he is sent off to school, is put through the routine of grammar and book-work, and the natural freshness and vigour of his inquisitiveness soon begins to fade away. After a time he ceases to take any interest in natural objects; his leisure is no longer given to nature but to athletics, and the spirit of inquiry is deadened altogether. The boy is considered to be much improved because he is less troublesome to his elders, but one half, and that the most active and educable half, of his mind is suppressed. This is the first result of 'a liberal education.'

The reader who has found himself able to agree with the arguments put forward—and if he disagrees it is to be hoped that he does so 'as the result of rational conviction, not of traditional prejudice'—will have come to the conclusion that he must agree with the demands made by Whewell fifty years ago, and quoted at the head of this essay. He will then ask what practical steps can be taken to meet the demand. Here we are confronted with the *non possumus* of the public-school master. You admit, he says, that classical teaching is essential; how are we to add Science to it? Even now the burden of things necessary to be learned is too great. After many years of teaching there are but few boys who have made any great progress in Classics, and if you add Natural Science you will break down the educa-tional machine altogether. Besides which, he will say, there are schools in which Science is taught, and you declare that the results are unsatisfactory. Yes, we have said that the results are far from encouraging, and this may be attributed to the fact that where Science is taught, it is made wholly subordinate to the Classics. Too little time is allotted to it; the marks obtainable in the Science classes and examinations are so small that a boy's place in the school is scarcely, if at all, affected by them ; too little provision is made for practical teaching and laboratory work ; and, finally, too much is attempted in the way of detail, especially in the early stages.

The first demand, then, is for more time for Science. How is this to be given without taking it away from classical studies ? The answer is that, under present methods of teaching, an enormous amount of time is *wasted* over classical studies. By improving the methods of teaching, as much and more Classics than are now thought necessary might be learned in little more than half the time now devoted to them.

Let us consider what a boy *does* learn at a public school. He arrives there at the age of thirteen or fourteen, after some five years' education at a preparatory school. The teaching in preparatory schools has been so much improved of late years, that a boy is already tolerably well educated. He has a fair knowledge of elementary Latin and Greek, he knows the rules of Arithmetic, has learnt some Algebra, and at least the first book of Euclid. In fact he is not far below the standard required for Responsions. In the four or five years spent at a public school he learns rather more Latin, rather more Greek ; he may make a little more progress with his Algebra, but he seldom gets beyond the second book of Euclid. Can it be said that those educational methods are entirely satisfactory which produce so very small a result in so considerable a time? It has been the conviction of the writer, ever since he passed from classical into scientific hands, that if classical masters only had the advantage of some scientific training, they would teach their subject more scientifically, and would thereby save ample time for the requirements of Natural Science.

But at the most, one can only expect a very gradual reform in the methods of classical teaching. The older masters cannot be expected to change long-established habits ; even the younger ones would find it difficult, and the only hope is from those who are coming on. At a time when the methods of education are becoming a special subject of study, will it be too much to ask prospective schoolmasters to study scientific methods and to try to learn something from them? In the meantime, while reform is gradually making its way, we want some opportunity of teaching Science in schools. An opportunity can be found which will not involve any serious dislocation of existing arrangements. It would appear that the study of Mechanics, because of its certainty and precision, is one of the most suitable subjects for elementary scientific instruction. There is no need to insist on the connexion between Mechanics and Mathematics. A considerable part of mathematical teaching might be made auxiliary to the study of Mechanics, with the happiest results for both. The algebraical problems which are commonly set for solution are too often trivial and unmeaning : boys take no interest in them, and will not make the mental effort necessary to solve them. But they will generally take some interest in working out the numerical results of an experiment which they have themselves performed, and in doing it they will at once exercise themselves in mathematical rules and reasoning, and will learn the value of Mathematics in the natural sciences [1].

But one of the greatest obstacles to effective scientific education in schools is the very small proportion of marks allotted to Science. A boy's place in the school depends primarily on his Classics, to a less degree on his Mathematics, and scarcely at all on his Science. And since boys are quick to see where they can save themselves trouble, they will

[1] 'The first four sections of the Physics Syllabus . . . constitute a course of practical Arithmetic and Geometry exercises, and give infinite opportunity for problems on ordinary surroundings.

'The graphic and experimental work in the Syllabus is intended to serve as an introduction to Physical Science, bearing in mind its necessary co-ordination with general mathematical work.'—The Incorporated Association of Head Masters : extract from the Report of the Committee on Science Teaching.

not make an effort which brings them no corresponding advantage.

Another difficulty confronts the Science master, in the fact that classes are arranged according to merit in Classics, so that both competent and incompetent boys are pushed through the same scientific course together, and proceed from lower to higher studies in accordance not with their scientific, but with their classical abilities. So long as this course is persisted in, a graduated scheme of scientific instruction is impossible, and the whole level of teaching is kept down to those who either cannot or will not work well at the subject. The remedy for this is simply better organization, the details of which would vary with the special circumstances of each school. But in every case proficiency in Science should be made to count heavily in determining a boy's place in the school.

Let us suppose that objections have been overcome, and that the schools are ready to make concessions to Science. We must consider what subjects may most profitably be taught, and how they should be taught. Though there is a divergence of opinion amongst scientific men on this point, the writer, who is himself a biologist, is convinced that a scientific training should begin with the study of the rudiments of Mechanics and Physics, and should continue with the study of the elements of Chemistry. It would take too long to urge all the reasons which may be brought forward in support of this view, but the following argument quoted from Whewell may suffice to convince all but the most prejudiced persons: 'No ideas are suited to become the elements of elementary education until they have not only become perfectly distinct and fixed in the minds of the leading cultivators of the science to which they belong, but have been so for some considerable period. We should by no means be in haste to adopt into the course of our education all new discoveries as soon as they are made. They require some time in order to settle into their proper place and position in men's minds, and to show themselves under their true aspects; and till this is done we confuse and disturb, rather than enlighten and unfold, the ideas of learners by introducing the discoveries into our elementary instruction [1].'

It is because the principles of Physics, and in a less degree of Chemistry, are so well established and so free from perplexity and indefiniteness, that they are most suitable for the beginnings of a scientific education. For the opposite reason the study of Biology is not so desirable as a commencement, though the study of the morphology of plants and animals, with as much vegetable and animal physiology as is necessary for the elucidation of the morphology, may be introduced with great advantage at a later stage. Physiology, pure and simple, is best avoided; for its principles are still involved in some doubt

[1] *The Philosophy of the Inductive Sciences*, vol. ii. p. 520.

and obscurity. And since modern Physiology is almost entirely dependent on Physics and Chemistry, a thorough knowledge of these must precede the study of Physiology. Similarly in Geology little progress can be made by the student who has not mastered the elemental ideas and principles of Physics and Chemistry and of animal and vegetable Morphology. (It may not be out of place here to caution teachers against the early use of that collection of miscellaneous information which is termed Physiography. After looking over some thousands of examination papers on this subject the writer is convinced that, unless it is backed by a sound elementary knowledge of Physics and Chemistry, Physiography is a subject highly hurtful to sound habits of thinking and reasoning.) As to how the rudiments of Physics and Chemistry should be taught we have an excellent indication in the report of the Committee on Science Teaching of the Incorporated Association of Head Masters. The report in question is something of the nature of a protest against elementary scientific instruction as it has been hitherto conducted. The proper objects of an elementary scientific education are clearly expressed in the following passage :—

' The exercises are arranged so that the pupils may themselves discover the facts and be led to formulate definitions, and this they should be encouraged to do in every possible way, that they may become acquainted with some of the fundamental properties of matter and with fundamental natural laws; and that they may be led to understand the reasoning used in deducing definite conclusions and generalizations from the results of their own observations and discoveries.'

The pith of the whole matter is contained in the last sentence. The object of elementary education is not to impart information, but to improve the under-standing, and the weakness of public schoolboys is that they have crammed up the information but have not got the understanding.

The second grade schools are leading the way; may it be hoped that the public schools will follow their example? And let it be noted here that every objection commonly urged by public schoolmasters may be met by reference to the secondary schools. Science teaching is too expensive; the secondary schools, which are poorer, contrive to meet the ex-pense. It is difficult to keep discipline in large practical classes; the secondary schools have solved the difficulty. There is no time for the work; the secondary schools find the time. The strongest argument which the public schools can adduce in favour of retaining the existing order of things is that, after all, they only profess to prepare boys for the Universities, and so long as the Universities do not require elementary science there is no reason why the schools should provide it to any greater extent than they do now. The answer, of course, rests with the Universities, and it is obvious that nothing will be done until Oxford and Cambridge are awakened to the fundamental importance of Natural Science as a part of a liberal education, and insist upon a knowledge, however elementary, of Mechanics and Physics in 'Smalls' and in 'Little-go.' If once they take this step, the public schools will be bound to follow suit.

In conclusion, it may be observed that it is not much to the credit of the older Universities that they are among the last to acknowledge the place of Science in a liberal education. In writing on the relations of public schools to the Universities it had almost been forgotten that public schools also pre- pare a number of boys for the Army. Quite recently the authorities have made Science a compulsory subject in army entrance examinations, a decision which will affect the question of Science-teaching in public schools to a considerable degree. As things now stand, it appears that the conception of a liberal education is different for the Army and for the Universities. The former requires Latin, a Modern Language, Mathematics and Natural Science. The latter require Latin and Greek with very little Mathematics, no Modern Language, and no Natural Science. The superiority seems to lie with the Army in spite of the absence of Greek. Lastly, the Universities, which are the leaders of intellectual opinion, should look to the changes which the spread of education is introducing among the people. Everywhere we see technical schools and schools of

Science springing up under the auspices of the County Councils and the Science and Art Department. The spread of scientific education is universally applauded, and it is the hope and conviction of many that it will enable us to stall off the competition of our great commercial rival, well-educated and scientific Germany. When the nation at large is making a special effort in the direction of a particular kind of education, it behoves the Universities to consider whether they too should not take their share in the movement, and lend their authority to the growing conviction that the Natural Sciences have an undeniable right to a place in a good general education, an education which shall extend and strengthen a man's understanding and fit him for the work which he will have to do in the world.

G. C. BOURNE.

THE TEACHING OF MODERN LANGUAGES

In the following remarks I am speaking of the study of modern languages as it forms a part of a school curriculum. My object is to state plainly what, in my view, can be accomplished in a public school, the lines on which the instruction should be given and the difficulties which at present stand in the way. But before doing this, it is necessary to refer to some erroneous notions or half-truths which are apt in this question to obscure the real points at issue.

First, we are often told that it is impossible to teach modern languages satisfactorily in a public school, or that, under ordinary conditions, it is so difficult a task that it is not worth while to attempt it, seeing that the knowledge of them can be readily acquired by a short residence abroad. This is a doctrine which is no doubt largely encouraged by the present unsatisfactory state of modern language teaching in our schools and the narrow and one-sided view which is often taken of the objects to be aimed at. The success of a boy's schooling in French or German is liable to be put to a test which may be very misleading. He is taken abroad, and is found perhaps incapable of making any practical use of a language which he is supposed to have been studying seriously for several years. Too often the fact is that he has actually learned nothing; but even where this is not the case, the test would fail to show anything but that he had no conversational power. On the other hand, the test is generally applied in such a superficial way that the display of a few phrases borrowed from a hand-book of conversation is taken as a proof of a real knowledge of the lan-guage. But we need not inquire how the view I speak of has arisen, or with what motives it is fostered: it is certainly held and published, and there is just sufficient truth in it to make it entirely misleading. On the one hand, it is true that to give boys at a public school a fluent and accurate conversational power over a modern language is practically out of the question; while on the other hand, it is not true that this power can be acquired by a boy of ordinary abilities during a short residence in a foreign country, or that it can be acquired at all without either long residence or considerable application. By a few months' residence in a family abroad, and without special study, a boy may pick up a few phrases of ordinary conversation, and acquire sufficient of a courier's knowledge of the language to make himself more or less independent of an interpreter in passing from one continental hotel to another; but to be able to speak with any degree of fluency or correctness on general topics demands not only at the very least a year's residence, but also systematic instruction and considerable industry.

Now it is well known that the instruction which a pupil gets when he takes lessons abroad is exactly of the same kind as that which is given, or can be given, in any one of our public schools at home. The professor in whose hands he places himself lays stress upon grammar, gives rules, sets exercises, hears translations, exactly as the language master does at a good school. The difference is that the student resident abroad may be presumed to be in earnest in his effort to master the language and devotes his whole energies to it, instead of dividing them among half a dozen other subjects; and that he spends twenty or thirty hours a week upon it instead of three or four. The only positive gain, though it is no doubt very great, lies in the opportunity of speaking the language at all times, just when work and interest are entirely centred upon it. The particular point, however, upon which I wish to insist is that the systematic instruction I referred to is indispensable, or at any rate that the only possible alternative is a residence of years instead of months; and that this systematic instruction can be given for the most part previously at the public school, and, if so given, will shorten by at least two-thirds the time of residence that would otherwise be necessary to give a full command of the language.

The ground that is covered in several years by lessons of two or three hours a week may be covered no doubt in a few months when the pupil gives his whole time to the study; but it is precisely in the work of laying the foundation that temporary concentration is least successful; the knowledge of inflections and constructions can be got in a very short time, but the ready use of them comes only with long practice. This fact is nowhere better appreciated than amongst the foreign professors who undertake the tuition of boys resident abroad; they are the first to recognize the value of previous school training, knowing very well that it is indispensable for the progress of their pupils.

Next, as to the method of teaching a modern language, a great deal is said which may be true enough in theory, but is altogether misleading in practice. We are advised, for instance, to follow the method of nature. We are told that a child acquires its mother tongue without the painful and laborious process of learning inflections, conjugating verbs, and applying rules of grammar, and that we must do away with this process as useless and obsolete. Partly as a consequence of this view, though partly, no doubt, on account of the prevalent superstition that any process that is valued as a means of true mental culture must of necessity be prejudicial to commercial interests, the educational world has been deluged with a host of new methods of learning languages. It is just possible that some of these may have a value for the private student; but they are in general quite unsuitable for school work. The majority of them have much the same relation to the study of languages as a ready reckoner has to the study of arithmetic. In some preparatory schools of an inferior kind, where these methods are adopted, it is notorious that no solid progress is made, however much pupils and parents may be delighted with the parade of a few common phrases, and that while no conversational power of any real value is acquired, the groundwork necessary for a thorough knowledge of the language is neglected.

The truth is that the revolt against the grammatical method is utterly unreasonable. There may be grounds for the complaint that in some fields it has been pressed to absurd limits; that boys have been made to learn lists of peculiarities and irregularities that have little to do with the standard usages of the language; that they have been overdone with rules and hampered with pedantries. But this is not a reason for discarding grammar altogether, for studiously keeping back from the pupil, for example, a declension or a conjugation of a regular verb, and requiring him to pick up the knowledge of inflections piecemeal, as the words are presented in reading or in conversation. Paradigms and simple rules of grammar are expedients which have been devised to save time and assist the memory; they are part of a scheme for improving upon nature. No one has yet suggested that we should discard the use of maps in teaching geography, or that we should abolish all artificial methods of classification; and yet to with-hold from the pupil the classification of words, schemes of declensions and conjugations and rules for construction, and leave him to the so-called natural method, is on a par with an attempt to teach geography by giving a detailed account of isolated places just as they happen to be met with in reading, without supplying any general groundwork of knowledge as to their situation or their inhabitants. It is true that in course of time, if the education of the individual is continued as long as the education of the race, the pupil must learn to generalize from particulars, and the fuller and wider knowledge will come. It is the order of nature; but what a process to start in the public schools of the nineteenth century!

Assuming then that the teaching of modern languages may be profitably undertaken in English schools, not only for the sake of literary culture, but with a view also to the easy and rapid acquisition of a command over them which will have a commercial value; assuming also that for school purposes we cannot set aside and can hardly hope to improve upon the grammatical method, I turn to the main difficulties which have hitherto prevented the attainment of a high general standard.

The first difficulty is that the study is not taken seriously enough. Years ago, we know, the French lesson was associated with lessons in dancing and deportment, matters which were not regarded as a part of the real business of school work. The traditions of those days still survive. Very few schools even now, except those which prepare largely for the Army or the Navy, set about teaching modern languages in earnest. In the preparatory schools, with some exceptions, the teachers, instead of preparing the ground and laying some solid foundation of definite knowledge, fritter away the time in teaching boys to say in French or German, 'How do you do?' 'What o'clock is it?' 'Pass the mustard, if you please,' and the like, before they have learned even such beginnings of grammar as the conjugation of the verbs *être* or *haben*. Most boys enter the public school practically destitute of grammar. As the result of a long experience of examining boys on entrance, I estimate that fully four out of five would make some mistakes in the verb *avoir*, and nearly half would make mistakes throughout. The state of things in regard to German is still worse.

It is urged of course that the credit of a preparatory school rests on the classical teaching, and that while Latin and Greek command the situation, little time can be spared for modern languages; but my complaint is not so much of the amount of time given as of the way in which it is used. Public opinion and common practice require that French should be taught in preparatory schools; a couple of hours every week are assigned to the subject, a master is told off to take the lessons, and there the matter often ends: no one seems to care what is taught or how the instruction is given, except perhaps in the case of a promising candidate for a naval cadetship. It is well understood that no boy who can do decently in Latin and Greek is ever rejected at the public school because he knows no French. I have known of a boy who learned German for a whole year at his preparatory school, I believe paying an extra fee for the privilege, and who during that time had been set to do literally nothing but practise the German handwriting.

The lack of real interest of which I have complained in the preparatory schools is almost equally conspicuous in the public schools, except where there are large army classes. Indeed, I think it might fairly be asked how far the disposition of boys to make light of their modern language lessons, which is notorious enough in many schools, is traceable to the indifference with which the subject is often regarded by the masters as a body. But even the most zealous teachers are sadly handicapped by the absence of any general standard of previous training. They find that while one or two boys in their class have been well taught, the rest not only are without any reliable knowledge, but often have a distaste for systematic work—the outcome of a preparatory treatment in which they have been flattered or amused instead of made to learn. The time allotted to the subject is necessarily limited ; the grammar has to go to the wall ; it is impossible to insist upon accuracy. The slovenly work which is the result is a disgrace to English education, and itself reacts upon pupils and teachers alike to diminish still further their interest and to extinguish their enthusiasm.

The first need then is that the study of modern languages should be taken up in earnest and treated systematically. This can only be brought about by a general lifting of the standard to be aimed at, by the general insistence upon the same accuracy and definiteness of knowledge that is looked for in the treatment of Latin and Greek.

Next, I believe that, in the early stages, the modern languages should be taught by the form-master. Apart from any question as to the success or failure of foreign masters in dealing with English public schoolboys, there is a distinct gain in making modern languages a part of the ordinary form-work—a gain in the thoroughness and soundness of the work as well as in the economy of time. All schoolmasters know very well that, in the case of young boys, much subdivision of work into special classes is a mistake; the difficulty of keeping in touch with a boy's work leads to loss in disciplinary control; and the subjects that are cut off for separate treatment lose in prestige. But, in the case of languages, there is a peculiar disadvantage in confining the lessons to three or four fixed hours. Grammar cannot be learnt by the hour; it requires the drill-work of short lessons of a few minutes each day, so that what is learnt may be kept always fresh in the mind by constant questioning and frequent practice in applying rules. It is only the form-master who has opportunities of doing this. In the more advanced stages the objections to special masters for modern languages are less serious, while the difficulty of securing form-masters who are competent to teach them as part of the regular form-work is much greater.

The importance of improving the standard of modern language teaching has been urged recently, chiefly because it is becoming more and more evident that the knowledge of French and German has a commercial value. We are said to be losing our commercial supremacy, and one cause assigned is our ignorance of foreign languages and our dependence upon secondhand information obtained through foreign clerks and interpreters. No doubt this is a matter of great national importance; but I consider that the strongest reason for pressing the question at this time is the interests of education itself. The great problem which confronts the schoolmaster in the development of modern education is how to retain, in the department of literary culture, something of the accuracy and definiteness of the old classical method, while widening the range of studies in the direction of science, and, in the case of the less able boys, avoiding the severity and the barrenness of a purely classical curriculum. Modern languages, if taught systematically and with a view to a high standard of style and accuracy, would, I feel convinced, admirably supply what is wanted. Their importance in the Army Examinations has, in some places, led to the adoption of more rigorous methods of teaching them, with the result that there is now plenty of evidence to show that when the same systematic course of instruction is followed, the educative capacity of the study of French and German is of exactly the same kind as that of Latin and Greek. As is well known, with many of the strongest supporters of the old classical education its peculiar value lies, in the case of boys of average ability, not so much in the knowledge imparted as in the system of instruction which I have spoken of as the classical method. It can hardly be doubted that the disappearance of this method would be disastrous for education generally. By grafting it upon the modern languages we should be not only retaining its disciplinary virtues in schools where they are most needed, but also doing the very best thing for the advancement of the study of the modern languages themselves. Unfortunately in many modern and technical schools the present tendency is distinctly in the opposite direction. Modern languages are left to be dealt with in the slovenly fashion to which I have referred; and Latin, if its prestige as an instrument of education is still strong enough to give it a place in the curriculum, is reduced to the same condition by the abandonment of rigorous methods of instruction.

It is, however, very much easier to point out shortcomings than to see from what quarter the impulse in the direction of reform is to come. The Universities at present have but little opportunity of exerting an influence in the matter, but even where they might help to set a higher standard, as in the case of the Certificate Examinations, they are apparently content to accept the existing state of things. Particular schools are doing something; but it can only be by awakening the interest of the teaching profession as a whole that any real and general improvement is to be expected.

A. E. ALLCOCK.

THE TEACHING OF MODERN HISTORY

THE study of Modern History has now been admitted to our schools and has taken a prominent place in our scheme of general education. The object of this paper is to consider whether, by improved methods of teaching or a more systematic organization, we can make it more worthy of the place that it has won.

Before, however, we discuss the question, it may be a help to consider what Modern History can do for us as a school subject, and what it cannot do. It is an excellent means of giving 'information,' of awakening interest in men and books, in life and politics; but as a class-subject taught to schoolboys it can never be a wholly satisfactory instrument for the discipline and training of the faculties, and it cannot, as is sometimes imagined, usurp the part which linguistic studies and pure mathematics play in education. The reasons for this are not far to seek; for while it is easy to discover whether the learner has 'got up' certain definite dates and facts, it is extremely difficult to induce him to use his own intelligence and to endeavour to reason about these facts. And in preparing his history lesson a boy

M

rarely uses anything but the tabulated 'causes' and 'results' of some abstract or the note-books of his instructors. From this it follows that if the limitations of Modern History as an instrument of school education are not carefully remembered—and many examiners seem to forget them—boys are encouraged to be 'wise with but little reflection,' which leads to a peculiarly unpleasant form of mental conceit.

But if the learning of Modern History at school does not give mental training, it has many other good results. It gives various interests to boys, encourages them to read, opens inquiries and studies which they often pursue with success for themselves when their school days are over; it provides them with a knowledge of ordinary facts and with general notions of chronology, which are just as necessary for an intelligent enjoyment of life as are the facts of arithmetic; it explains to them what 'history' means, and how it is written, and prevents them from imagining, like Mr. Tomlinson in *Scenes of Clerical Life*, that 'history is a process of ingenious guessing,' or that a statement in a guide-book is a proof of the founding of Glastonbury Abbey by St. Joseph of Arimathea.

If we inquire how the general course of historical study in a school should be arranged, the answer will probably be as follows: 'The teaching must be systematic and in accordance with a consecutive scheme, so that the learner, gradually working through one period after another, may, when he leaves school, have at least some acquaintance with the whole of English history and with the outlines of continental history; while his knowledge will be continuous, and without gaps or lacunae.' This view sounds eminently reasonable; but when we proceed to draw up our scheme and work it, difficulties present themselves which are not easy to solve. The time which can be devoted to Modern History is limited; if large spaces are to be covered each term, the information must be meagre, the text-books lifeless. Is a boy never to study minutely any stirring epoch? Are the men and women of whom he reads to remain mere names, shadows, without flesh and blood? A further question also suggests itself—Who is to teach the subject? Is it to be the form-master, or is a school to have specialists in the subject on its staff?

This last question goes to the root of the matter. If the general organization of the school permits the history teaching to be handed over entirely to specialists, the systematic method may work very well; indeed, in many girls' schools it has been extremely successful; for the specialist has enthusiasm and knowledge, and makes the dry bones of the text-book live. But in boys' schools it is the general opinion that a boy (more especially a young boy) should do as much work as possible with his form-master; and if this system be pursued, the most carefully drawn-up scheme is likely to be a failure. The form-master, whose main work is linguistic, may not care for history; he may have little or no time for reading it (and unless a man is learning himself he can hardly expect to teach), or even if he does read it, he will naturally confine his studies to the periods which he finds specially interesting. These cannot always coincide with those that he is expected to teach, and a man who has an intimate knowledge of the eighteenth century may be quite at a loss if you turn him on to the Heptarchy or the Angevin kings. And so there is a danger that the history lessons may become dull things without savour or salt, and degenerate into mechanical attempts to exact from the boys names and facts which they do not understand or assimilate — a worse than useless proceeding.

Seeing then that there are serious objections to the adoption of either system in its entirety, the way of safety lies, I think, in some form of compromise. The following suggestions occur to me :—

A date card, or rather a short book of a few pages containing the chief dates, names, and facts of history, should be in use throughout the school. Portions of this book should be assigned to each form, and it would be the form-master's business to see that this special portion is learnt, and the back work carefully revised from time to time, until at last the boy knows the whole book as he knows his Latin grammar. If the school is fortunate enough to possess a specialist, he might occasionally give a lecture to several forms combined, taking the book for a text.

In addition to this, each form should read some one work that deals with the subject in much greater detail; and a wide discretion in the choice of periods and subjects should be left to the form-master.

Moreover, there are some books which boys like, which may be said to 'teach themselves,' or, as schoolmasters say, are 'quite successful.' These should be read at frequent and definite intervals. Among such books are Collier's *Great Events of History*, Seebohm's *Protestant Revolution*, Morris' *Age of Anne*, Frederic Harrison's *Cromwell*, Macaulay's *Essay on Lord Clive*. One or more of these books should be constantly used throughout the school.

It will also be found useful occasionally to prescribe the same subject or period as part of the term's work for every form. If this is done, boys are led to talk about their history lessons to their friends in other forms, to take sides on a question, and to read for themselves.

The mention of books leads us on to consider some of the practical details of teaching.

The proper choice of books is an important matter, and a very difficult one. The object is to get a book which a boy likes, and which he will go on reading for himself after he has finished his allotted task. It is hard for a man, even if he knows boys well, to tell what they will like; to know their dislikes is a simpler matter. A boy is catholic in his tastes; all the books in the list I have just given he would—with

his love of 'under-statement'—describe as 'decent':
he is not put off by a florid style; on the contrary, he rather prefers it.   He does not object to a
king 'wading through blood to a throne,' or to 'the
Ambrones and Tigurini joining their Celtic war-
scream to the deep-bayed battle-cry born of the
trackless forests of the Elbe.'   But if he does not
want style, he insists on vigour, picturesqueness, and
power of presentment, and generally recognizes such
a master-hand as Mr. Harrison's, if he is given the
chance.   He does not like books of compressed
facts—a sort of historical pemmican; if he were
ordered to 'get up' the late Professor Freeman's
General Sketch of European History, he would, like
the man who 'read *Clarissa* for the fable,' feel
inclined to hang himself.   On the other hand, he
dislikes books where description is displaced by
disquisition.   He has no excessive love of imparti-
ality.   He hates being preached at, being patronized,
talked down to, told the same thing over and over
again.   He prefers the 'drum and trumpet' presentment of history, and (like most of his elders) takes
little interest in the growth of institutions.   You
may tell him that if he studies the constitutional
relations of king and Parliament, he will see 'how
Englishmen learnt to keep their own money in their
own pockets'; the prospect does not attract him;
indeed, he probably will consider such a course
of action mean and uninteresting, being of what
Mr. Bagehot calls the 'cavalier or enjoying tempera-

ment.' If you talk to him of constitutional history, he is apt to behave as Dr. Johnson did on a famous occasion, 'withdraw his mind and think about Tom Thumb.' He agrees also with Dr. Johnson and with Lord Monboddo in esteeming biography and the history of manners as the 'most valuable'; and it is for this reason that most small boys prefer the time-honoured Mrs. Markham to any other English history-book.

In their preference for biography and manners, boys, I believe, are right. Constitutional study is not suited to the young; for, as Aristotle says, τῆς πολιτικῆς οὐκ ἔστιν οἰκεῖος ἀκροατὴς ὁ νέος· ἄπειρος γὰρ τῶν κατὰ τὸν βίον πράξεων. A boy can 'get up' and reproduce tabulated answers about the *Curia Regis* or the Privy Council, but he rarely understands them. Let him leave such studies until he is in the Sixth Form or has left school, when he can read great books for himself. And if we must teach him about institutions, would it not be well first to see if we cannot get him to understand something about those institutions under which he is at present living—how his town and parish and county is managed? If a boy is studying the Middle Ages, let him hear a good deal of its art, manners, and literature, and let tallages and knight service and statutes of mortmain take a modest place in the background. Perhaps the most futile thing of all is to make children repeat 'political definitions'—'What is a king?' 'What is a charter?' 'What is the meaning of *de haeretico comburendo?'* Children, if stupid, repeat such things by rote; if intelligent, they translate them for themselves into a dialect they understand, like the little girl who defined a charter as 'a thing which kings had to sign when they were naughty.'

It seems now hardly necessary to emphasize the fact that Geography is the handmaid of History. But the youthful fancy does not lightly turn to atlases; and indeed but few of their elders, when they read history, follow Sir George Warrington's example, and 'take the tattered old map-book from the shelf, and see the board on which the great contest was played.' It could be wished that in England we had better maps and plans of battles and historical atlases than are at present obtainable; in this respect we lag sadly behind the Germans.

The mention of plans of battles suggests another question:—Should military and naval history be taught? and if so, in what detail? The decision had better be left to the idiosyncrasy of the teacher. Some masters dislike the whole subject, asking with Thackeray—

> 'Tell me what find we to admire
> In epaulets and scarlet coats—
> In men, because they load and fire,
> And know the art of cutting throats?'

Others have neither the knowledge nor the skill which such studies require. One thing seems certain: you must either deal with such subjects fully and with

some interest or leave them alone altogether; a perfunctory or meagre treatment of them is worse than
useless. 'A cursory relation of such a struggle as
Magenta or Sadowa is simply unintelligible. We
cannot comprehend what caused the failure of the
attack on the redoubt, and the practical success of
the advance *en échelon*; how it was that the right
centre found itself compromised about three in the
afternoon, and why it should not have experienced
that sensation an hour earlier or two hours later[1].'
One campaign or one battle only in each term should
be studied in detail, for the rest we must content
ourselves with the results. The text-books often
make this mistake, they give either too much or too
little, and they are sometimes carelessly written; for
instance, to say that the French at Waterloo 'saw
the Prussian army *coming down the road*' is a misleading way of describing three army corps coming
into action. Personally, I think every boy should
study some military history: it interests him, it is
an excellent intellectual training, since the least confusion and vagueness is fatal, and to understand the
various phases of an engagement and their connexion
(especially in a naval action) requires some grasp
of mind. Finally, I think it highly important that
a battle should not be regarded as a sort of large
football scrimmage; for 'the English have a notion
that generalship is not wanted; that war is not an

[1] *A Holiday among some Old Friends*, by Sir G. O.
Trevelyan.

art, as playing chess is, as finding the longitude, and doing the differential calculus are (and a much deeper art than any of these); that war is taught by nature, as eating is; that courageous soldiers, led on by a courageous wooden pole with cocked-hat on it, will do very well [1].' Now, a boy naturally does regard a fight as a kind of football match; and before we begin we must try to clear his mind by a few preliminary questions. Such might be: How much space will an army of 20,000 men cover when posted for battle? What length of road will they occupy on the march? How many miles can an army march in a day? What is the meaning of a 'base,' 'lines of communication,' 'key to a position'?

As to the various accessories which are now frequently used to assist the teaching of history, such as magic-lantern slides and collections of prints and photographs, they are, like lectures, most excellent and helpful things, provided that they are kept in their proper place, and not allowed to become a substitute for hard reading and oral teaching.

A very short experience of teaching will show a man how much patience it requires (to use Dr. Johnson's phrase) 'to rectify absurd misapprehension.' He will find in some of his pupils an extraordinary confusion of mind which leads them to make statements which would be irritating if they were not amusing. One kind of confusion comes from the

---

[1] Carlyle's *Frederick the Great*, vol. iv. p. 88.

fact that young boys read much more slowly and incorrectly than grown-up people imagine. This frame of mind can only be left to Time the healer. A second kind is rather creditable to the boy. He hears, or comes across in his text-book, some words which he does not understand, but which he explains mentally in some way satisfactory to himself. His intentions are good, but the results sometimes amazing. For instance, in reply to the question, 'What were the causes which led to the Declaration of American Independence?' one answer given was, 'The Americans wanted to send all their parcels to England without putting stamps on them: of course we were not going to allow that.' Or again: 'When Rodney saw the French he sent for the weather-gauge, and, when he had looked at it, determined to break the enemy's line.'

If a man cultivates clearness of thought and expression, encourages his pupils to ask for explanations, and shows his disapproval when they allow anything they do not understand to pass unquestioned, most of these confusions will disappear. Some must remain, and I should expect a set of examination papers completely free from confusion to be devoid also of any spirited and original answers. It would mean that the keen historical enthusiasts at the top of the form had been sacrificed to the duller boys at the bottom; and to say that 'there was some confusion in the minds of the weaker boys' is like ending an account of a mile race with the remark that 'several of the inferior runners were some little distance behind the winner.'

Yet one more question arises in this connexion. To what extent should the teaching be purely oral? I believe that one of the most serious defects of English education is that there is far too much dictating by the master and writing from dictation by the boys, and not nearly enough viva voce questioning and answering. The results of this are to be seen, I think, in some of our national deficiencies. 'Conference maketh a ready man'; but as a nation we are not ready. A lecture should be spoken, not read; a history lesson should differ from a dictation lesson. A master, having thought his subject out, should go into his class-room and talk to his boys. He will flounder and hesitate; but the class will listen with an attention and interest which his most carefully-written statements will not secure. For the boys feel that they are listening to something at first hand; they are possessed by some faint reflection of the spell which binds the audience to an actor or an orator. Then questions and explanations on both sides must follow, and the boys must be encouraged to speak, not in single words and phrases, but at length. Care must be exercised in reading extracts from books, as boys unfortunately regard the reading of anything as an interval during which they can relax their attention. Prolonged reading is a mistake, unless it be interrupted with numerous questions and illustrations. Short notes may sometimes be a necessity, but the greater part of each lesson should be devoted to the spoken word. The practice of using no book and dictating lengthy notes to small children seems ridiculous in a country which possesses printing presses. If these notes are not carefully corrected, they are worse than useless; on the other hand, the correction of them is an intolerable burden upon the teacher, and may rob him entirely of time for reading, thinking over, and preparing his lessons.

We must, however, obviously vary our methods of teaching with the varying ages of our pupils. These we may classify very roughly as follows :—

1. Boys under fourteen and a half in preparatory schools, and the lowest forms in public schools.

2. Boys under sixteen, who are below the Fifth Form.

3. Boys from sixteen to nineteen, who are in the upper part of the school.

As regards the first of these it may be said that children in England are generally made to read and write a great deal too much. Boys of this age are 'breaking their brains' over the elements of Latin and mathematics. Their history lessons should be of the nature of a relaxation, intended to interest, not to train. They are keen to know, their memories are at the most retentive stage, and they will remember any number of facts which are put before them in a picturesque way. They should have no preparation, and little to do with books; if they must have a text-book, let it be of the old-fashioned kind —

Mrs. Markham or Miss Sewell's *History of Greece.* It is at this age that the most skilful teaching is required, for the master will have to follow the example of the Jesuit fathers and the teachers of the lower forms of the German *Gymnasien*, and learn how to tell a story and teach without a book.

In the second stage the main object must still be to interest and inform; but something more is now necessary. The boy must be taught how to read a history book, how to grasp the salient points, to perceive the connexion of events, their causes and results.

When a boy has entered the Fifth Form his history work assumes a different and more serious character. He should now work, not at text-books only, but also at classics, such as Macaulay's Essays or Burke's Speeches, or biographies, such as Mr. Harrison's *Cromwell* or Professor Laughton's *Nelson.* He will now be taught to make 'notes' for himself, will show up an abstract of a few pages of Macaulay, will have it returned to him corrected, and receive a fair copy. He will write essays and be shown how historical subjects should be treated. His form-master will encourage him to read for himself by explaining what books in the school library bear on the term's work, and will occasionally set him a paper of questions which will lead to a little elementary research in great books. He will try to show him also why history is studied, how histories are written, and what historical research means;

the value of monuments, of documents and memoirs; what an historian is, and how a true historian is not only an antiquarian, but also a man of letters; how such an achievement as the *Decline and Fall of the Roman Empire* takes rank with great discoveries in natural science; how histories, as Bacon says, 'make men wise.'

In many schools now there are generally some boys who are 'specializing in history.' This 'specializing' has its own dangers; any boy who does so should continue some of his classical work, especially his Latin prose, and make a serious study of some modern language, German for choice. He should be kept away from small text-books, and work through Gibbon and Mommsen, whose last two volumes on the Roman Provinces form the best of introductions to the history of modern Europe and Western Asia. He should have as much viva voce work as possible.

One final suggestion may be permitted. It will be found profitable to have in every school a small committee of such masters as are interested in history teaching, who will manage the competitions for special history prizes, keep an eye on the general history teaching of the school, and have some supervision of the school examinations in history. A dull or carelessly set history paper may do serious injury both to teacher and learner. To ask a boy to 'give an account of the Wars of the Roses,' or to 'describe Wellington's operations in the Peninsula,' is to reduce the whole thing to an absurdity. A convenient form of paper consists of two parts :—(1) A number of questions on dates, facts, and names to be answered in one or two words. (2) Two or more questions to be treated fully. The first part should only occupy a third of the time allotted to the whole paper.

That a schoolmaster should be an ideal history teacher is impossible ; for the ideal teacher of history should, among other things, have been a cabinet minister, a soldier, and the chairman of a county council, have examined terriers and extents like Mr. Round, and have received a banker's training like Mr. Bagehot. But the teacher of history in a school should possess some power of lucid exposition, and some skill in telling a story ; he should sympathize with boys, and be not entirely destitute of a sense of humour. He may be an antiquarian, but he must avoid pedantry *sanguine viperino cautius*; he may have his pet characters and theories, but his private enthusiasms should be tempered with discretion ; he should believe in his subject and its power to make boys happier and wiser ; finally, when he ceases to be a learner of history, he should cease to teach it.

C. H. SPENCE.

'AH, my boy, you learn history, do you? Well, here's sixpence for you if you'll tell me the date of the battle of —— ' ' Please, Sir, we don't learn dates of battles.' ' You don't! My boy, here's half-a-crown for you.' This is an Oxford story told of Charles Neate. It might well be whispered as a sibylline precept into the ear of some of the teachers of history in our public schools. In a typical paper set recently to Sixth Form boys the first question is, ' When and with what results were the following battles fought?—Brunanburh, Tenchebrai, Lewes, Towton, Nancy, Pavia, Lepanto, Rossbach, Lutzen, Lexington, Sluys, Sobraon, Austerlitz, Valmy, Camperdown, Sadowa, Wörth.' Question (2) is, ' What events are connected with the following places?' Question (3), ' What do you know of the following?' (a list ranging from the Peace of Wedmore to Grattan's Parliament). Question (4), ' Who were (Bede ... to Cavour)?' and so on with the rest of the six questions. No doubt the boy who does the best in such a paper will be the best read and probably the ablest boy. But for all that, it indicates a false conception of History. History is not, even in its most rudimentary form, a fortuitous concourse of names and dates; nor ought the human mind even in the schoolboy to be taught to measure its powers by the number of these items that are found arbitrarily adhering to it.

It is not too much to say of such a paper, as illustrating some of the present teaching of History, that it is not teaching, and it is not History. What History is, and what it ought to be, are questions that have been answered in many different ways; but one thing at least is certain, that it is not and ought not to be this collection of dry bones. The teacher's function is to make dry bones live, and not to hold them up in this way for study in their most desiccated and most osseous condition.

It may possibly be argued that such a paper represents not what is taught, but what is 'examined.' But examination that does not guide and direct teaching, that tests not the powers of reflection or of expression but mere brute memory, that tries to reduce History to the parrot processes of learning by heart from which even Grammar is struggling free, such examination deserves some of the strictures that Mr. Auberon Herbert passes on all examination.

The fact is that, paradoxical as the statement may seem, History is at once a necessary part of education, and a somewhat unsatisfactory subject; unsatisfactory, that is, as a mental training. Treated as it often is, History is too 'easy' a subject. 'I took it up because it could all be read in an armchair,' an ingenuous student has been heard to confess. It ranks among what Americans call 'soft options.' To read Macaulay 'with half an eye' may unnerve a boy for the sterner stuff of Classics or Mathematics.. At best, it leans too much upon mere memory. It seems to require little mental effort; it might be defined as a smooth tale, generally of war. A good teacher indeed will soon show the beginner that this is not really so; he will rouse him to analyze, to criticize, to recombine for himself. But even then the fact remains that History demands judgement, experience, tolerance; whereas the schoolboy 'demands emphatic warrant,' black or white, angels or devils.

On the other hand, some study of History is indispensable on any theory of education. It is indispensable as a means of giving life to the other subjects of study. What a mental awakening it is when first 'that hated people, the ancient Romans,' become living credible men in the pages of Mommsen, or when the Middle Ages, instead of mere bigotry and barbarism, become warm flesh and blood in the persons of St. Francis and St. Louis. The beginning of all mental growth is the stirring of the imagination, and this must inevitably be stirred by the story of Hannibal or the story of the Syracusan harbour, even as told in the arid school-books of the last generation.

Some study of History is also indispensable in another way as a part of liberal education. Some general idea of the world of the past on which the present is built up ; some sense, however dim, of the continuity of national life ; some conscious- ness of the great inheritance transmitted from past generations to be handed on by us unimpaired to the generations to come,—all this may be regarded as a necessary part, if a hitherto neglected part, of the moral equipment of a civilized man.   We can measure its value by the mental blank pro- duced by its comparative absence in some Colonial or New World communities.   Englishmen them- selves are often by foreigners accused of 'insu- larity'; and there seems no sufficient reason why English schools should not include in their curriculum, as German schools do, some outline at least of the past history of Europe and the great conceptions of the Middle Ages.   It is said, again, that no one is so ignorant of the institutions under which he lives as the average Englishman. This is not merely an anomaly; we are used to anomalies.   But it is a social danger in a country whose empire and whose future under democratic institutions and socialist panaceas must depend on its powers of self-government.   To put schoolboys through a course of Constitutional History is not desirable and not necessary ; but to give them some elementary idea of our actual institutions, to enable them to regard a newspaper as something more than a mere 'vehicle' for cricket news, is desirable and ought not to be impracticable.

It may be said that this sort of thing is very fine in theory, but that what schools have to look to is results; they must keep their eye on the examinations for scholarships, for certificates, and for matriculations; and what tells in these examinations is accurate and copious knowledge of facts, the sort of knowledge for which there must perforce be a great call upon the memory. But this argument also is a mistake. It is in truth the old conception of History over again, which sees in it little beyond names and dates, a mass of chronological details. To be stuffed with this would certainly be the very worst training for the examinations in view. Those tutors who have to take University students through the course for the Final Schools of History either at Oxford or at Cambridge would above all things deprecate premature specialization. The best lawyers are able men who have taken up law last, and the best historical student will be the one who has had the widest and soundest general training. So much is this felt to be the case, that out of twenty-seven teachers of History in Oxford, twelve have taken the Final Classical School. The most generally acknowledged defect of 'History men' is a want of that exactness which is connoted by the word scholarly. A clever boy, however decided his bent towards History, would do well not to specialize at all upon it, even in Oxford, until he has had the thorough drill of Classical Moderations. As to the Certificate examinations, the line they have taken for many years and the results that have followed show a steady progress from the mechanical to the intelligent modes of studying History. The papers set have tended less and less to encourage the mere accumulation of facts, and more and more to require some intelligent handling of them. Better text-books are used; there is more practice given in the way to answer questions; Geography is less neglected; above all, there is evidence of more oral teaching to supplement the books. As to History scholarships, there are now ten or twelve offered in a year instead of only one or two. This has led to a large increase in the number of candidates, though not to a corresponding increase in the number of candidates of real ability. Incompetence in Classics is too often taken at school as giving a presumption of future success in History. It has therefore seemed worth while to ten of the Colleges at Oxford to issue a joint notice that these scholarships are awarded on promise rather than for bulk or range of knowledge, and to come to a joint agreement as to the general lines of examination. It is agreed to lay most weight on the essay and general papers, which test natural ability; to give opportunity for the display of scholarship in any of the languages (Greek, Latin, French, German); and, finally, in the History papers proper to give a wide choice as between Ancient or Mediaeval or Modern History, and as between English or Foreign. The practical effect of this agreement seems hardly to have been yet understood in the public schools. It opens History scholarships (1) to any boy who has ability up to the usual scholarship level, (2) to any boy whose ability is less in the direction of Greek and Latin composition and more in the direction of essay writing, literary criticism, and the other subjects which are often conveniently, if oddly, grouped under the term 'English.' More than that, it does not in most cases require that a boy shall have turned aside from his ordinary school course; he can stand on his essay, on his reading of such general books as Macaulay's Essays and Bagehot's English Constitution, and on the amount of History, Ancient and Modern, that he has already done for Certificates. No special 'cramming' is needed; or rather special cramming would probably defeat itself. Among candidates who have been elected within recent years, and whose after-career has amply justified their election, there have been some who omitted several of the papers, others who had worked only at Ancient History, others again who had studied only the history of Literature, and so on; not to mention candidates who had at school been comfortably marked off as stupid. That there should be exact uniformity in the details of all these scholarship examinations is not of course to be expected, nor is it desirable; but there is enough to be of very sensible convenience to teachers.

There is another examination in which History plays a large part; that for admission to the Home,

Indian, and Ceylon Civil Services. Since the new regulations that came into force in 1892, University men (and Oxford men in particular) have formed the largest proportion of those selected. Men of anything like first-class ability can take this test in their stride, that is without modifying or interrupting their regular course of reading for the Final Schools. This is particularly true when they are reading for the Final Classical School. But to a considerable degree the man reading for the Final History School is also very favourably situated. He has more or less in hand, so to speak, five or six of the eight or nine subjects required to give reasonable prospects of success. He has English Composition, English History, Foreign History (a selected period), Political Economy, Political Science, and either French or German; if he has taken honours in Classical Moderations, as he should have done, he has his Latin and his Greek Language and Literature; and he probably has done enough either of Roman or of Greek History to make up a ninth subject.

This scheme implies that he has a year to spare after his Final History Schools, i. e. that he takes his Final Schools before he is twenty-two; i.e. that he leaves school as soon as may be after he is eighteen—a point that it is important to remember. But so long as he remains at school, the most 'paying' thing he can do is to get the best he can out of the ordinary public school curriculum in Latin, Greek and French ; to 'make the best of himself all round,' as it is expressively put. The Indian Civil Service examination was once supposed to be the happy hunting-ground of the 'crammer.' Putting aside the delicate question, Where does 'successful teacher' end and 'crammer' begin ? it is certain that an examiner who cannot discriminate between 'cram' and genuine work does not know his business. This certainty and the number of different subjects that have to be well digested and assimilated, together with the working of the skilful rule of inverse deduction of marks, combine to defeat both specialism and superficiality and to make thorough grounding a *sine quâ non.*

It appears then that the various external examinations to which the schools do and must look for their reward, ought not to be regarded as having any narrowing or cramping effect. The schoolmaster is free to teach what history he pleases, to teach it in the way he finds most stimulating, and to teach it with the conviction that what is best for the general development of the pupil's mind is best also for the pupil's chances in the future.

The rest of this paper may be devoted to a rapid sketch of the practical suggestions that experience forces on the mind of a teacher of History who is also led as an examiner to observe and compare the results effected by the methods of other teachers.

The most important thing for the proper teaching

of History is to secure the proper teacher. Here and there may be found a genius who can teach a subject without having ever had a methodical training in it himself. There have been, and perhaps still are, remarkable examples to be found of great success of this kind. But there are many more cases in which a master has found such greatness thrust upon him, and in which to the very end he never quite achieves it. Broadly speaking, it may be said that the days of History as an 'extra' are over, the days when it was left either to any one master who had some time to fill up, or to each master to manage as best he could in his own spare time. No school can now be regarded as fully equipped which has not at least one teacher who has been through a regular historical course, who is qualified to speak as an expert on the subject, and to direct, supervise and report on the work which is being done in it throughout the school. Such a man need not attempt to do all the historical teaching himself, but he can do much to guide it and to stimulate it by moving round the different forms, on the German plan, by delivering occasional lectures to each form or to several forms together, and by taking special charge of boys who have distinct aptitude for the study or who are preparing for special examinations in it. He cannot well have studied History himself without acquiring a deep sense of its fascination and its dignity; and some reflection of that which he feels deeply himself must have the power to interest and to stir any generous young mind. A man may indeed have the loftiest conception of History and the soundest views upon it, and yet be unable to teach it. But this criticism applies to all teaching; and it only goes to strengthen the argument for a systematic training of teachers in general. It may be advisable however, as a counsel of worldly wisdom, for one who wishes to introduce a new ideal of History teaching in a school, to present himself with credentials of having learned 'pedagogic' as well as History. Such a man, well arrayed for his enterprise, furnished with a knowledge of the new methods by which historical inquiry is beginning to open out a new world before us, commanding a field in which boys revel after their drudgery of Grammar and Euclid, such a man has a lot which many a teacher might envy, and a task which is its own reward. He will soon discover how small a part of his work can be done for him by any text-book; not 'the written word' (as Plato says), but living speech alone can give inspiration and real guidance. The text-book only gives information, and at most a few suggestions; and it was a wise man who said that if there was any one thing he despised more than another it was information. When the pupil has 'got up' a prescribed chapter in the book, when he has the necessary outline of names and dates, then comes in the real lesson. He is questioned on what he has read, made to analyze his facts, to recombine them under new headings, to detect where gaps have been lightly bridged over and where difficulties lurk, to shape for himself the questions which go to the very heart of the matter, and to attempt to give his own crude answers.

There is however a better method still, but one which has not yet been thoroughly organized and applied. It would be based on the principle of proceeding from the known to the unknown, from the concrete to the abstract, from the particular to the general. Given an intelligent boy of ten or twelve; he is to take up the history of his country from B.C. 55; what is the best way to begin? The ideally best way would be to show him Housesteads on the Roman wall, with its paving-stones furrowed by the soldiers' feet and its gate-posts worn deep where the men on guard sharpened their knives on them; to rebuild, as it were, before his very eyes the strenuous crowded life of the camp and the meaning of that wonderful barrier, the *murus* and the *vallum*, in their sevenfold completeness; to let him hear the sentries pacing from guard-house to guard-house, the orders passing along the covered pipeways from mile-castle to mile-castle, the legionary carts rattling along the military road from camp to camp; so to make him feel, as we feel that which we see and hear, what a Roman province and what the Roman empire really was; and finally what its downfall meant, by the charred floors, the huddled skeletons, the broken weapons and ornaments on the very spot. But it may be objected, οὐ παντὸς ἀνδρὸς ἐς Κόρινθον: we cannot all go to Borcovicus. Ten years ago such an objection would have had weight. But photographs and guide-books, relief-maps, and plaster models and casts, autotypes and facsimiles of coins and antiques, have brought Roman remains and many other things to our own doors. I should like to see in a school the creation of a historical museum, which should contain a set of appropriate instruments for the study of each period. Such things as the following may be suggested: for example, a relief-plan of a section of the Roman wall, as now standing, and as it was when intact; the same for the Roman villa at Chedworth, the Roman walls and gates of Chester, and a piece of Roman road; a large scale-map of the neighbourhood, with all Roman names and remains clearly marked in red; figure-models to illustrate Roman warfare, military and naval, Roman siege-craft, and Roman encampments; some practicable Roman swords, *pila*, eagles; a ground-plan of the legions located in Britain, and the evidence inscriptions supply as to the wide variety of races and religions embraced in a Roman army.

There is another method of working from the known to the unknown, and that is to take a familiar institution like the House of Lords, or an obvious fact like the differences as to race and speech between Kent and Devon or Sussex and Yorkshire, and to work backwards to the germ of the institution or the primary historical cause of the differences, stopping at the landmarks on the way; e.g. Kent as it is now, Kent in the Civil War and the Wars of the Roses, Kent with Wat Tyler and against William the Conqueror, Kent as a vassal kingdom of Wessex and of Mercia, till we reach Kent under Æthelbert and the story of Hengest. This method needs the knowledge of what to leave out, and is a little exposed to the danger implied in reading history backward, the danger of unduly simplifying the problems, and encouraging a habit of mind that may become priggishness. But as an occasional exercise it is invaluable; it never fails to awaken interest, and it forces upon the instructor the paramount virtue of absolute clearness of view.

Connected with the method of working up to the general from the particular, is the use of biographies. It cannot be too much insisted on that this is the proper way to introduce a beginner to any new period. It is the meaning of the 'tell us a story' instinct, so strong in the young. It is the only form in which they can get their first grasp of new times, new countries, new ideas. A boy who at sixteen has read with appreciation Oman's *Warwick* and Creighton's *Wolsey* is in just the right state of mind to go further and to appreciate still better a more advanced and more detailed view of the fifteenth and sixteenth centuries. He has begun to feel that History is human, and he will meet with a healthy resistance any misguided attempt to force him to a diet of Constitutional History. Constitutional History is too abstract, too dry and innutritious for boys ; it lends itself to 'cram,' and without a good general knowledge behind it, it is a vain thing.

Mediaeval and Foreign History have the merits of being stimulative and attractive ; but they must be studied either in broad outlines on the plan of such a book as Bryce's *Holy Roman Empire,* or in a detached fragment, preferably biographical, like Church's *Anselm* or Comines' *Memoirs.* Otherwise the multitude of new names and places and the interlacing of the various threads are hopelessly distracting.

It is very essential to have some training for the reasoning and reflective powers to counterbalance the purely historical work ; and in this light the preparation required for the 'General Paper' as set in scholarships is invaluable. This paper too is found by experience to supply with the essay the safest test of natural ability, as distinct from mere cubical capacity on the one hand, that is the capacity for holding information, or on the other from mere facility of flow. A candidate elected on his purely historical papers sometimes turns out a disappoint-ment ; one elected on his general papers and essay, rarely so.

Another thing that ought to be made more use of than it is now is Geography, including in that term not merely the accurate locating of a list of places or the jotting down plans of battles, but the application of physical geography, and practice in drawing sketch-maps. Taken in this latter sense, it proves always an attractive subject, especially when explained by a teacher who has some faculty of constructive imagination, to enable him to trace out the part played by geographical conditions in the making of states. An admirable example of what can thus be done is seen in Michelet's well-known *Tableau de la France.*

Practice in writing answers to questions is also one of the most important and withal one of the most neglected points in historical teaching. Think of the time that is devoted to acquiring the art of writing Latin prose, that is, a piece of Latin just tolerably correct as to grammar, but little above the canine in structure and in idiom. Pupils require rigorous criticism, not merely to learn how to write English, but to learn how to set down a good answer to a question, even when they have the necessary knowledge of facts. Such an answer must be strictly relevant, fairly complete, and not confined to one issue ; it must avoid mere narrative, it must have a sort of 'plot,' it must be terse and pointed, and yet free from slangy, trivial and colloquial expressions ; it should strike a key-note at the outset and reach some kind of a conclusion at the end ; it should steer between vague cloudiness and overloaded detail. 'Enough, you convince me no one can be a poet.' Yet, in sober truth, answers are constantly being sent up which do actually combine these merits.

To write them does indeed demand a certain natural instinct for style and a natural justness of view; but it demands also careful training, trenchant criticism, and occasional study of good models. The improvement made in a short time by a clever boy under these conditions is sometimes quite astonishing. Boys, again, soon see how effective a use may be made of memorable sayings, of striking quotations, of significant facts and illustrations generally. Some pedants seem to think truth is own sister to dullness. But what can serve as a better example of what historical writing ought to be than some of the masterly and brilliant paragraphs in Ranke, especially in his earlier work? It is nowadays almost compromising to refer to Macaulay; his sins as a historian may be deemed unpardonable; and the magic wand of his style may be too perilous for any to handle. But in some respects he has unique value for teaching purposes. It was not without justice he boasted that he never wrote a sentence that was not clear; he has an extraordinary power of attracting and fascinating young readers; and he possesses in perfection the great art of making a general statement by presenting it in its most telling individual case. 'He (Bacon) indulged in no rants about the all-sufficiency of virtue. . . . He dealt not at all in resounding nothings, such as those with which Bolingbroke pretended to comfort himself in exile, and in which Cicero vainly sought consolation after the loss of Tullia.' 'Such a book might be light reading in the days of Hilpa and Shalum.' 'The disappointment of Falstaff at his old boon companion's coronation was not more bitter than that which awaited some of the inmates of Rheinsberg.'

Finally, it is important to acquire, and only by practice can one acquire, the art of doing one's best 'to time'; the art, that is, of writing a full and adequate answer, say in half an hour, with no aid of books and notes. For after all, in this bustling world promptitude counts more than accuracy; and to be *doctus cum libro* avails little under the ordinary conditions of life.

Even the taking down of notes from a lecture or a book is a matter that cannot be left to the light of nature. There is no magical efficacy in the mere act of writing down sentences dictated by a 'coach'; on the contrary, it has a servile and deadening influence. It is better to take down only headings and salient points, filling in afterwards by reminis-cence. This trains the memory to act retentively and by selection, until the selective process can be carried on during the actual lecture. The note-book should be an aid to memory, but not a substitute for it. Young students are nearly always too wordy in what they take down; they copy when they ought to rearrange, and substitute manual labour for mental. Few things are so pathetically ludicrous as the note-books of a docile beginner.

Text-books are an ever-recurring problem to the

teacher. He must be content to remember 'the best in this kind are but shadows'; and his imagination must mend them. It is often necessary to combine them, taking up one for part of the subject, and a second for a different part. It is always necessary to supplement them, and this can best be done by referring to extracts from the original writers. There is an excellent series of these in German and in French, and something of the same kind in English (in the little books called *English History from Contemporary Writers*). It is some comfort that the kind of text-book in which 'every female bosom thrilled at the handsome figure of the Young Pretender' has been driven out of the better schools by the various manuals written by Bright, Gardiner, York Powell, Tout, Oman, and Ransome.

It is not superfluous to end with the caution that what is wanted is not infant historians, still less prodigies of memory, but well-educated boys, able to think clearly and to write well, with scholarly minds and sound taste, generous and broad in view, interested in the world of the past and appreciative of its great men and great deeds, and so the better fitted to learn their own part and take their own place in the present. There is in the young a great fund of latent interest, and even enthusiasm, ready to be enlisted in the right cause, and no study is so well adapted as History to draw out and utilize this force.

A. L. SMITH.

THE TEACHING OF ENGLISH
LITERATURE

In writing this article it has been my object to approach the question from the point of view occupied by a master in a public school. And I will concede at the outset that my remarks and suggestions are the outcome of aspiration rather than of experience. At the present time English literature can hardly be said to form a part of the regular course of study in our public schools. And yet there is some reason to hope that we are at last beginning to recognize that it is a possible and desirable element in secondary education. For while the purely classical curriculum, which characterized our public schools thirty or forty years ago, has been so far modified and expanded that education to-day is in danger of becoming too broad and shallow instead of too narrow and too deep, there is yet an impression widely prevalent that there is still something lacking in the intellectual equipment which we provide. The best authorities in our schools and universities are unanimous in their complaint that boys in our public schools grow

up strangely ignorant of and indifferent to the
history and beauty of our national literature. They
read it little and study it less. Even in the
holidays they rarely settle down to enjoy a book
of real merit, and they certainly know less of our
great authors than do their contemporaries in the
schools of France and Germany.

Who is to blame for this? Not the publishers.
For there are innumerable editions in the market,
educational and otherwise; selections, abridge-
ments, prefaces, glossaries, and annotations stream
out of the press every year. We have our penny
poets and penny novels. Everything is done to
make the path of literature cheap and attractive.
Public opinion is not to blame. The growth of
free libraries and the interest taken in such competitions as the choice of the best hundred books
indicate a sympathy as widespread as it is genuine.
And yet our boys for the most part remain
serenely indifferent to it all.

We may indeed regret this state of things, but after
all the reasons for it are not far to seek. To read
and enjoy literature demands leisure and quiet, and
there is little of either in the public schools of to-day.
In a former generation I think it can hardly be
questioned that the abler boys read more by
themselves than they do now. The hours of work
and play were not so elaborately organized and
filled up. School life offered far fewer distractions
and attractions. There was no gymnasium, no

music school, no workshop ; to say nothing of
the insistent and irresistible athleticism which has
in recent years assumed such stupendous proportions, and which apart from the hours of actual
play absorbs such an immense time in looking on
at games and in mere conversation about them.
Fashion is omnipotent, and a boy must have not
only a strong literary taste but also an independent
character who has the courage and originality to
strike out a line for himself and evince a preference
for the milder pleasures of literature.

But it is not only the athletes and their clients
who are open to this impeachment. It is equally true
in another way of those abler boys whose bent lies
rather in the direction of science and mathematics.
To many of them literature is as distasteful as music
is to those who have no 'ear.' They have no turn
for general reading, no desire to cultivate the
power of English composition, no acquaintance
with the great masters of prose and poetry. The
whole subject is often viewed with supercilious disregard as a waste of time.

To some extent this is the result of the premature
specialization which our scholarship system has engendered. And until recently the Universities, and
especially perhaps Cambridge [1], did little to discourage it. Fortunately, however, there are some signs of
a change in the right direction, and it is satisfactory

[1] It is fair to admit that English essays have always formed
a most valuable element in the Oxford system.

to note that even at Cambridge an English essay is now to be required in many of the principal College and University Examinations. And if report speaks true, the corrective was sorely needed. The singular essays contributed by many of the candidates have proved conclusively the necessity for this reform.

I do not forget that at Cambridge there is the Mediaeval and Modern Language Tripos, and at Oxford the School of English Literature. But they have not as yet exercised any tangible influence upon school teaching. Boys cannot be expected to add the knowledge of Anglo-Saxon to their other studies, and though, as the late Professor Freeman used to insist [1] the Universities are probably right in requiring a thorough knowledge of language as a basis for the study of literature, yet the schools are compelled to take a humbler and more restricted view of the subject.

But it may be asked, why expect from athletic and unimaginative boys an interest in an intellectual exercise for which they have no natural disposition? Studies, and especially literary studies, which are pursued against the grain, are of little value and leave but a transient impression. Where the sympathies are not engaged, the memory is asleep. Why not allow boys to follow the pursuits which nature dictates? Have done with this artificial

[1] See his article on 'Literature and Language' in the *Nineteenth Century*, October, 1887.

stimulus, this pedantic expectation of the impossible. The ordinary John Bull has no turn for literature. He is practical, observant and dutiful, but, like George of Hanover, he does not greatly care for 'boetry' and 'bainting.' He has no ear for the beauties of rhythm and the niceties of a perfect style. Literature, like sketching, is more adapted for his sisters than himself. It is something if he reads anything. Let him read what he likes. Give this one the *Field* and that one a volume of the *Badminton Library*, and let us be therewith content.

Now this of course is an agreeable view of education. It is more common than is supposed, and follows the line of least resistance. And yet those who believe in the ennobling effect of good literature, who are conscious of the profound debt they owe to it, who know by experience how it can leaven thought, character, and feeling, and who are intensely reluctant to see the spread of a mechanical, material, and unimaginative spirit in education, are not minded to surrender thus unconditionally to the Philistines. In spite of opposition and indifference, the cause of English Literature seems worth fighting for. We affirm that no education is complete without it, that though a minority with a strong literary taste can take care of themselves, yet the majority may and practically do grow up with little if any knowledge of the subject; that if the seeds of it are sown wisely at school they will produce an invaluable harvest in the later years, and that we have no right by our negligence to debar the next generation of the pleasure and profit which such a study can promise.

And when we think of the immense possibilities which lie before the English language, and remember that, so far as human prescience can forecast, it is destined to be the predominant language among mankind, and when further we reflect how many influences are at work to debase its original purity and dignity, it appears to be one of the first and natural duties of education to protect the best traditions and encourage the study of the highest models.

But to descend to humbler and more practical ground, it seems more than ever needful now to make such an effort in our classical schools. For there is a real danger that the study of the classics will gradually be so smothered by a dry compost of archaeology and philology that their original charm and freshness may be effaced. We live in an age of notes and facts. There is a tendency to disparage any knowledge which does not lend itself readily to examination. But boyhood is the period of imagination, and of the two perhaps the dry bones of erudition are more injurious than the flowers of rhetoric. For anything which tends to encourage the professional rather than the human element in our teaching is a matter for regret. It is, as every teacher knows, far easier to impart facts than to inspire feeling and fancy, but in the process a melancholy transformation often supervenes, and you find too late that what was meant for bread is after all no better than a stone.

Now, narrow as the old classical course was in old days, at least it provided an adequate *literary* training. There were many things omitted and neglected, but owing to the careful and frequent practice of composition in prose and verse, a classical scholar left school well exercised in the choice of appropriate diction and the power of expression. He also acquired some facility in original composition, and by that close study of a passage of poetry, without which a translation from English into Latin or Greek verse is quite impossible, he became intimately familiar with many of the finest pieces of English literature. But the writer of Latin verse has few admirers or supporters now.

> ' The bigots of the iron time
> Have called his harmless art a crime.'

It has long been the fashion to pour scorn on Latin verse; but there is much caricature in the criticism, and it would not be surprising if its claims as a vehicle for literary training were accorded a new hearing and granted a new lease of life under slightly different and more sensible conditions.

Nor was it merely Latin verse which served as an implement for literary distinction. Fifty years ago there was far more attention paid to the rules and methods of original composition in prose. It is fair to say that it was in Latin, but that does not interfere with the argument. The point is that boys were taught how to treat a subject, how to arrange their thoughts in an orderly form and in due proportion, how to present their arguments for and against a proposition, and how to sum up a question at the close. The essay was obliged to follow some such outlines as these :—*Propositio, Ratio, Confirmatio, Conclusio.* In a word, the simpler rules of rhetoric were taught. We may smile at them now, but the result was that instead of producing the amorphous and ill-digested essays we are too often accustomed to now in public schools, there was some effort made to inculcate the proper methods of thinking out a general question and expressing the result in a satisfactory manner.

But the pendulum has swung far, perhaps too far, in the opposite direction. The practice of Latin verses and Latin essays is being gradually consigned to the limbo of antiquated methods, and is never likely to be revived, at any rate on the old scale. But their disappearance has left a blank, and I am not sure that we have even yet furnished an adequate substitute for them. One such substitute however, and to my mind the most satisfactory, may be found in a more systematic study of English composition. By English composition I do not mean merely the elements of grammatical analysis and sentence-structure. This is very useful and necessary so far as it goes ; much more attention is devoted and rightly devoted to it than once was the case, and doubtless it forms the best and most scientific introduction to the study of Latin and Greek as well as of English composition ; for you cannot compose correctly until you have in some way learnt to distinguish between subject and object and predicate, and to master the simpler forms of substantival, adjectival, and adverbial clauses. But this is soon acquired by a little practice, and belongs to the teaching of elementary grammar. By composition I mean rather the regular exercise of writing English essays and even occasionally English verse, and I venture to urge that far more can and ought to be done in this direction.

The Greeks were fully alive to the importance of this branch of study, and it is a question whether much of the Greek literature, which is still accepted as the model and pattern of literary art, would ever have reached such perfection and maintained such a standard without the rhetorical labours of the sophists in the various lecture-rooms of Greece. The same remark applies to the writings of Cicero, Pliny, and Tacitus ; it is reinforced by the literature of the Renaissance ; and the French, who for generations past have been distinguished for the art of a precise and perspicuous style, have always insisted on a rigid standard of literary composition in their higher schools.

It has not been so with us, at any rate in our public schools. The subject has been sadly neglected. It is, or was till recently, quite common for boys below the Sixth Form to go through their school life without ever having to write an English essay at all. By some it seems to have been thought that boys could write essays by the light of nature, whereas there are few things which require more training, just as there are few which serve more effectively to elicit real ability. Others viewed the practice with prejudice and distrust, excited no doubt by a reaction against the foolish subjects set for essays to a former generation, or by a notion that boys should imbibe facts instead of expressing views, forgetting that a little care in the choice of a theme will meet the first objection, and that when the mind is thus fed exclusively on facts and rules, the faculty of original thought and expression is rapidly stunted and impaired.

And even when essays are set (I am speaking of public schools), they are often set in such a perfunctory way that they are of little use. A form-master perhaps thinks it is time to set an English essay for a change. After some cogitation he hits upon a thesis. This is given to the form without comment or suggestion or reference to authorities. The result is precisely what might be expected. It is a case of bricks without straw. The poor boy stares at the thesis till he is dazed, and eventually there emerges a disconnected *farrago* of scrappy remarks, like headlines in a newspaper, the thoughts unexpanded without any recognizable head or tail. The proper method is of course widely different, but it requires some previous care and thought. Just as it is impossible to correct a copy of Latin verses well without having made or studied a fair copy, so it is almost necessary to make a preliminary sketch of an essay to guide a beginner through the first difficulties. Not only so, but the essay should be on a familiar theme, and if possible connected with the other work on which the pupil is at the time engaged. Nothing is more fatal than to teach a boy to write glibly about nothing, to weave words without thought or substance. A boy's reading and experience is circumscribed, and he can only be expected to write on something with which he is already familiar. History lends itself readily for the purpose. Let us suppose that he has been reading the history of some great war, then he may be required to discuss some particular aspect of that war, a result which can only be obtained by taking a wide survey of the subject, by combining and rearranging the facts he has already learnt in his history. Such questions, it is true, are often set in Examination Papers, but then they are not criticized carefully afterwards, they are marked and thrown into the waste-paper basket, and the writer never has an opportunity of knowing whether they have been properly answered or no. Or again, if he is reading or learning by heart some piece of poetry, he may be requested to write an appreciation of the work, to sketch the plot of the story (it is astonishing how many boys fail to grasp any idea of the plot), to select the passages which appear to him most striking and beautiful, to discuss the character of the similes, and to compare them with those he has met with in other poets. If, however, some more general subject is selected, then an outline should be suggested and the beginner should be warned against the common faults, such as imperfect sequence of thought, obscurity, cumbersome sentences, disproportion and pretentious writing[1]. But after all the principal thing is to encourage a boy to *think*, and to express his thoughts in his own way. If there is evidence of thought, if the matter is good, even though the manner is disappointing, the essay should receive a generous meed of commendation.

And here I should like to interpose a few words in behalf of the composition of English verse. What has been said about the connexion between prose composition and the study of literature applies, though perhaps to a minor extent, to verse. Some of the time that used to be devoted to the rigorous study of elegiacs and iambics might now be spent on the explanation of English metre and rhythm, the laws of accent, emphasis, pause, alliteration, personification, and the treatment of metaphor and simile. None but those who have actually tried can tell how few boys are conscious of the metrical proportions of a line, and how difficult they find it in composing a simple copy of English verse to maintain from stanza to stanza the identity of the metre which they

[1] See Dr. Morell's *Practical Composition* (Simpkin & Marshall); Professor Nichol's *English Composition* (Macmillan).

have selected. I do not pretend for a moment that by this means we can produce poets. *Poeta nascitur non fit.* And yet, as Tennyson used to say, *Nascitur poeta et fit.* Much may be done (I have found it by experience) to elicit a latent gift of versification, and gifts are worth cultivating in default of genius ; even where they are wanting, a little practice in English verse arouses a new interest in the poetry which boys have to read or learn. If half the ingenuity and care that has been bestowed on the composition of Latin verse in such books as Mr. Ainger's *Clivus* were bestowed on a similar treatment of English verse, we should not, I think, find such blank indifference to the attractions of English poetry.

I have said thus much about English composition, as I wished to emphasize the importance of con-necting it with the study of English literature. But I must pass on to discuss more particularly the best methods of teaching the latter at secondary schools. And by literature I suppose we mean such books as appeal to our common humanity, to man as man. They must have the note of universality. They must touch our emotions, our common interests and sympathies. For this reason we may consider such books as White's *Selborne*, the *Compleat Angler*, the *Religio Medici* as literature in the sense of which I am speaking, even though they appear at first sight to be otherwise. For our purpose literature may be said to include all those works which serve to interpret human character and external nature, and which are written by acknowledged masters of the English language. So stated no subject could seem more attractive, and yet somehow, for boys at any rate, it remains a very difficult subject to teach, and by no means so popular as might be supposed. For instance, in the Higher Certificate Examination of this year, I notice that only half as many candidates took up English Literature as took up Latin, Greek, French, Divinity and History. In the Lower Certificate, on the other hand, the subject is far more popular, and this proves how little root it has taken in our public schools.

There are many reasons for this. To begin with, it does not lend itself readily for examination purposes or for catechetical teaching in form. It is less susceptible than classics of being studied in snippets. The classics indeed suffer, but not so seriously, as there is so much accessory matter in the shape of grammar, allusions, various readings, choice of words in translation, &c., which must be learnt if the teaching is to be thorough, apart from the comprehensive study of the work as a whole. It is not so, or not so to the same extent, in English literature. Here we do want to see the work steadily and see it whole, and to read it as the author wrote it. Take, for instance, such works as *Macbeth* or *Quentin Durward*. It is impossible to approach them like a book of Homer, a page at a time, with notes on verbal forms and grammatical construction.

This I know is occasionally done, but the result is a lamentable failure. At the end of a term's work the class know the notes and miss the plot. They have not seen the wood for the trees. The truth is that the book must first be read through continuously. And this is not very easy to arrange at school. It means that boys must be allowed opportunity to read it by themselves or that it must be read aloud in class, both of which occupy considerable time with little expenditure of effort. Boys will not take such work very seriously. It savours of dilettantism, and they are apt to pay less respect to it in consequence. Then there is another difficulty. There is no doubt that as a rule the taste for literature develops late. It is commoner at college than at school, commoner in later life than at college; I suppose because it requires leisure and quiet, and demands a wider range of reading and riper experience that can be expected in boyhood. I have purposely dwelt on these difficulties, as they are too often ignored, and consequently the subject is taught ineffectively or discarded in despair. What then can we do? Our ideal, I take it, is to try to implant and foster in boys a taste for reading the best literature, and so to train that taste as to wean them from the vagrant butterfly reading characteristic of the present day. But we must not expect too much. In this, as in many other paths of education, we may lead and we may guide, but we cannot drive. The taste must be a natural growth, and much of the seed we sow will fall on barren ground.

Learning selected passages by heart is such an obvious suggestion, that I need not do much more than mention it. And yet, perhaps it is worth while insisting on the value of the practice, as it is rather out of favour nowadays. To my mind it is a great mistake to neglect it. We can only learn by heart with ease at one time of our lives, and many a man has found satisfaction in repeating to himself passages which he learnt perhaps with painful effort in youth. They are priceless possessions for life. But it need not be said that no passage ought to be committed to memory without being previously understood and explained.

A good deal may also be done by offering prizes for voluntary study of the subject out of school. Some of the very best work done by boys is voluntary work. But such competitions do not of course affect the mass. We must not therefore be content with leaving it to voluntary effort. It should as far as possible form an inseparable part of our form-teaching in English history. There is, I am aware, a difference of opinion on this point. The late Mr. Cyril Ransome, for instance, deliberately eliminated it from his history. I cannot agree with this. It seems to me a travesty of history to teach, for instance, the Elizabethan period without reference to Spenser and Shakespeare, or the Age of Anne without reference to Pope. It is not too much to ask that one contemporaneous literary work should be studied in connexion with the period of English History learnt during the term. And it would be a great help to teachers if a series of typical literary passages in chronological order were published, to serve as a companion to historical teaching. In this way boys would gain some idea of the sequence and growth of literature, and how the characteristic features of each period were not the result of chance, but the natural outcome of previous influences. But I think it would be possible to go further than this. The subject lends itself readily to the lecture system. And it would be a good thing to organize lectures to sections of the school, or even to the whole school together. The fact is, it is a subject that requires an expert, an enthusiast, and a specialist to handle it properly, a teacher well equipped and thoroughly convinced of the value and interest of the subject. Form-masters have so many irons in the fire that they can hardly be expected to satisfy these require-ments. But it ought not to be impossible to enlist the service of a good lecturer. There are already some available in connexion with the University Extension System. By thus supplementing the teaching in form the boys would gain some familiarity with the names and respective dates of the great authors, and would learn to appreciate literary allusions which at present are hopelessly lost upon them. Such a lecturer could clothe the grammar of the subject with living interest by illustrative quotation and personal anecdote. To many boys no doubt the subject would still be unattractive. That is inevitable. But still I feel assured that there would be a handsome residue who would be tempted into a serious study of literature in later life.

Such a course of study begun at school cannot fail to touch the springs of character and affect the emotions and the imagination. It may not brace the logical powers or store the mind with useful information ; but education has many functions, and the discipline of the taste, the appreciation of perfect language, the contact with the greatest inter- preters of human feeling and aspiration, is no mean part of a liberal education, and will furnish in after years one of the best antidotes to the ennui of idle- ness, the mechanism of routine, and the exhaustion of overwork.

E. W. HOWSON.

II.

WHAT suggestions I can offer as to the teaching of English Literature are to be made from the point of view of an examiner. It is an established custom to speak of the examiner as the great hindrance to the intelligent teaching of English Literature. The thing needful, it is said, is to teach students to *enjoy* literature, to find their pleasure in reading master-pieces instead of in ephemeral publications, and enjoyment cannot be gauged by examination. Papers, however, will be set at the end of the school year, and teaching must therefore be directed to meet the only possible sorts of questions—questions in bio-graphy, or history, or archaeology, or folk-lore, or textual criticism, or grammar. To this complaint an examiner naturally replies that while he frankly admits that by the teaching of literature should be meant the teaching how to enjoy literature, yet this enjoyment must depend upon comprehension, since no reasonable creature can enjoy what he does not understand; and examination, while unable to gauge enjoyment, is able to gauge comprehension.

If the teacher still quarrels with the examiner, it is because they disagree as to what is implied in this term comprehension ; and so the following pages had best be used in making clear what that term implies at least to one examiner.

In a certain sense a student may be said to understand a play of Shakespeare who has looked out all the antiquated words in a glossary ; and in no sense can a student be said to understand a play who does not know the meaning of all the words in it. No doubt there is a certain pleasure to be derived from the mere sound and movement of such a verse as—

‘ The multitudinous sea incarnadine,’

but teacher and learner would be at one in saying that this aesthetic satisfaction—although in itself excellent and one of the things the teacher has to encourage—is not by itself sufficient for the appreciation of any poetical writer, except perhaps Edgar Poe. The words, then, must be understood. But when this is accomplished, and the play of Shakespeare is thus put upon a level, for ease of comprehension, with current literature, it is only then that the work of appreciation begins. I use the word ‘ appreciation ’ because it seems to express better than any other the kind of effort required from the mind when brought face to face with a piece of literature. I take it that English Literature is the record which the most gifted of our countrymen have left us of their highest feelings upon human life ;

a record that remains interesting for us because human life in its broad features remains the same to generation after generation. An individual work of literature represents the ultimate impression made upon the thinker's mind by some fragment of experience or some aspect of the world as a whole ; that experience may be a bird's song, or a patriot's death, or anything else that happens in the physical or moral worlds; and the work of literature aecomplishes its purpose when the impression of this experience is transferred from the poet's to the reader's mind, so that he sees the particular phenomena as the poet has seen them. It seems therefore to follow that the function of the teacher is to put the student at such a point of view that the work he is studying may make upon him the entire impression it was intended to make—a reflection of that in the writer's mind. He must clear away hindrances, stimulate interest, and direct attention.

I will say nothing here about the teaching of very young children. As an examiner, the lowest class I have had experience of is that which presents itself for the Junior Local Examination, i. e. pupils of about fifteen years of age, who offer a play of Shakespeare. Shakespeare is also the principal author read by candidates for the Senior Local and Joint Board certificates, so that it may be useful if I shortly explain what it is an examiner means by an understanding or appreciation of a play of Shakespeare.

1. The plot must be known. This, it may be thought, might go without saying; but experience proves that nothing needs saying so emphatically. This summer *King Lear* was set for the Joint Board Examination, and *Hamlet*[1] for the Junior Oxford Local; and a very large percentage of the Local Candidates, and far too many of those whose papers I looked over for the Joint Board, did not know how their play ended. In an examination on *Julius Caesar*, in answer to the question what part Casca and Cicero take in the action, I remember being told that the ghost of Casca incites the conspirators in the battle and makes them rush into the thickest of the fray, and that Cicero comes in at the end and helps to keep order. Such mistakes ought to be absolutely impossible. The mischief comes chiefly from using for school purposes editions furnished with notes. These, if I had my will, should never come into the hands of pupils, but be reserved like cribs exclusively for teachers. First of all, the very appearance of such books conveys to the child a false impression, for he jumps to the conclusion that what needs so much explanation must be intolerably dull; and, secondly, the notes occupying in his mind the position of honour, he prefers to take them solid as they stand without troubling about the text. I shall not be thought guilty of undervaluing the obligation under which Dr. Aldis Wright has laid all students of Elizabethan literature by his researches

[1] See below, p. 226.

into the meaning of words. But when the notes are, as in his famous edition, purely philological, at the hands of an incompetent teacher the im‑pression may be conveyed that the chief reason for reading Shakespeare is to learn the life-history of such expressions as 'hurly-burly.' Not that the child at the time resents this; he would far rather learn any number of pages by heart than give his mind to understand a scene of a tragedy[1]; but the result of such note-cramming is seen in two ways, immediately when he takes the play as read, and afterwards on leaving school when he puts away his Shakespeare with his school-books. The class-book put into the pupil's hand should be a simple text, with at most a glossary; and he should be at once told to read it. Before the play is brought into class at all, it should be read and re-read and read again privately—what could be better for a holiday task?—until there is a very definite outline in the mind of what happens. It would not be amiss to let the class read, first of all, the story of the play in Lamb's *Tales from Shakespeare.*

2. When the outline of the story is known, atten‑tion must next be directed to the plot; if it be a tragedy, who the hero is, and in what the tragic

---

[1] A schoolmistress who succeeded to a class that had been in this way taught philology under cover of literature, told me how at first the class rebelled at being bothered with the text of the play, and begged to be allowed to go on learning the notes as usual.

situation consists. The student should be told that it is of the essence of tragedy for the circumstances in which the hero is placed to be such as to play upon the weak points of his character, and bring him to ruin. Thus, if the play to be read were *Julius Caesar*, the class would be told that the tragic interest is centred in Brutus, who is the type of a patriot perfectly noble and unselfish, and yet without insight into the needs of the time; and they would be stimu-lated to watch how this one great practical defect in Brutus brings on the catastrophe, first by allowing a base conspiracy to come to a head, and then by mismanaging things when the conspiracy had ap-parently triumphed. It would be well to read the play in class at first rapidly, an act at a time, for the sake of showing the development of the main action, and how each scene contributes to it. The teacher, for example, after the first scene had been read, would point out that it puts us in possession of the state of feeling at Rome after Caesar's triumph for his victory at Munda, and shows us that his absolute power, although offensive to the old re-publican magistrates, did not press heavily on the people. He would point out in the next scene that Cassius is the originator of the conspiracy, and bid the class notice his skill in angling for Brutus, whose reputation he sees to be essential for the success of the plot, compared with the rough and ready means employed for catching Casca. And so on.

3. When the play comes up for reading a second time, the teacher would naturally give closer attention to the dialogue. A question always on the teacher's lips should be, 'Why does X say that?' 'What is the object of the speech?' 'How is it characteristic?' It should be a first axiom that every speech is appropriate to the speaker, and should be recognizable as his and his alone by a person who knows the play; and it should be no less axiomatic that everything said is said with a purpose and reveals character. An examiner regards inability to assign characteristic speeches to their proper speakers as the next worse sign of failure after ignorance of the story. To say, for instance, that 'I am not Barbason, you cannot conjure me,' from *Henry V*, was said by Pistol to Bardolph, or by Pistol to Fluellen, or by Nym to Bardolph, is far more than a mere slip of memory. It shows that so well-defined a character as Pistol has never been realized. And yet may I dare to tell that in looking over for certificates papers already marked by teachers for school purposes, I have found a gross blunder like this considered so trivial that it is expiated at half a mark? At such times one wonders if the examiner is after all the only enemy that the teaching of literature has to dread. Again, to say, in answer to the question, 'Why does Shakespeare put such poetical speeches into Macbeth's mouth?' that a dramatist must put his poetry somewhere, while it displays an amusing wit, makes no less evident an

utter want of appreciation of Shakespeare's dramatic method. For some time past, however, the papers of the majority of candidates who offer Shakespeare in the higher examinations show that they have been very ably lectured on the more important persons of the dramas. Against this process of lecturing there is not much to be said (unless we reckon the boredom of the examiner, who finds an identical answer running with slight differences through a quarter of a hundred papers), always provided that the lecture does no more than put together what has been evoked in class from the play itself. But the valuable teaching as to character is that which is given by hints as the reading proceeds, and is not restricted to the major characters. Thus a teacher who pointed out, if we may recur to *Julius Caesar*, how Casca in Act i. scene 2 first echoes Caesar and then echoes Cassius, and how in the next scene he makes sudden discovery that he is a bondman, will have done more for his pupils' appreciation of this hero than by the most epigrammatic character-sketch, which would be taken down, learned by heart, tossed to the examiner, and then forgotten. Dr. Aldis Wright once coined the term 'sign-post criticism' as a name for the kind of criticism he thought well to forgo. For a scholar it is no doubt superfluous, but it is a kind of criticism of much value to young students. Let the teacher not be too proud to be a sign-post; to be for ever pointing the finger, 'notice this,' 'notice that.'

4. Explanation ·of difficult phrases is best given by the teacher shortly and *viva voce*, when they come up in reading the play; but of course there is advantage now and then in devoting a lesson entirely to such matters for more exact instruction. There cannot fail to be much in our older literature that needs explanation in regard to the manners and customs of the time. But here again a warning is necessary. It is not enough that the allusions be explained. These remain mere isolated facts of archaeology until the meaning of the whole sentence is seen in the context. For example, in *Henry V*, the Constable says of the Dauphin's courage: ''Tis a hooded valour; and when it appears, it will bate.' The student who has been informed that falcons used to be hooded, and when the hoods were removed they would 'bate' or flap their wings, has got hold of a more or less interesting fact, but has not necessarily any clearer comprehension of what the Constable thought of the Dauphin's courage. Similarly with historical references. When Sir Andrew Aguecheek exclaimed 'I had as lief be a Brownist as a politician,' he had some meaning, and this meaning the pupil should dis-.cover, or be told. But let an examiner set this passage for explanation, and this is the kind of answer he usually gets: 'Sir Andrew means that sooner than be a politician he would rather be a follower of Robert Brown,' which explains nothing, even though a long life of Brown be appended with

correct dates.. Far better be frankly unhistorical, with the young gentleman who paraphrased this sentence, 'I would as soon join the Browning Society as go into Parliament,' which is at least a sentence with a sense. One other point may be referred to under this head. It is right and proper to let the student understand that the Tudor way of treating classical subjects was to dress them up in the guise of the sixteenth century; and when examples of this treatment occur they will naturally be pointed out. But some pupils seem to imagine that the main purpose of reading Shakespeare is to expose his anachronisms. They are always scenting them. 'This play,' says one by way of summary, 'contains a few classical allusions and one anachronism.' On Antonio's speech in the *Tempest,*

> 'They'll tell the clock to any business that
> We say befits the hour,'

another sagely writes, as sole sufficient comment, 'An anachronism. There were no clocks in those days.'

It is my experience that comedies are generally less well known than tragedies. It may be that more time in class is allotted to the tragedy as being the more difficult, while the comedy is trusted to explain itself. But if so, the expectation is not father to the fact. A joke is pretty sure not to be understood. 'He that is well hanged need fear no colours,' set some years ago, was understood, if my memory serves, by less than one per cent. of the candidates for the Joint Board certificate. I suppose so trifling a pun is below the dignity of a Literature class. Not quite so fatal but still disastrous enough I have found Sir Toby's retort to Sir Andrew when he lamented wasting his time over fencing, dancing, and bear-baiting instead of spending it 'in the tongues,' 'Then wouldst thou have had an excellent head of hair'; and Stephano's proverb, 'As proper a man as ever went on four legs cannot make him give ground,' is sure to be met, outside one or two of the best schools, with what is considered the sufficient note, 'proper means handsome'; the notion of handsome men having four legs being accepted without protest or excuse. These are trifles, but I mention them for this reason. It needs no proof that if these trifling jokes had been explained to the class, they would never have been forgotten. The class would have been enraptured and conciliated by the thought that Shakespeare could make a pun. But the teacher, in the pursuit no doubt of loftier ends, had neglected his first plain duty of explaining his author's text.

It is a usual practice for examiners to test intelligence by giving a passage to paraphrase, and there can be no more comprehensive test devised. For a paraphrase makes clear not only whether the student understands the words and the grammatical construction, but whether he has appreciated, what is of more consequence, the beauty of the poetry. To some extent, then, the examiner can gauge 'enjoyment.' To paraphrase 'transparent Helena' by 'Helena, you are so thin,' or 'not all the water in the rough rude sea' by 'not all the seas in the United Kingdom,' is to fail in more ways than one. The common faults in paraphrasing are either a version so free that it avoids most of the difficulties, or one so close that it merely transcribes them. It is worth noting that familiar phrases like 'The quality of mercy is not strained,' or even 'To be or not to be,' are frequently not understood.

5. When the play has been read first 'in great swathes' and then piecemeal, it is well to go back and consider it as a whole, lest the general impression should be lost in the details. At this last stage the teacher can point out the unity of the drama, the interaction of the characters, the happy way in which the main and under plots are combined, and other points of like nature. Unless with very advanced and particularly intelligent pupils, it will be well to avoid any mention of the sources from which Shakespeare drew his materials. The fear of examiners who can found questions upon the learned prefaces of the editors causes time to be wasted upon imparting information which is not only beside the point but most distracting to nine children out of ten. I can lay my hand on my heart and profess I have never set a question upon the sources of a play of Shakespeare since 1886, except when such a question has been prescribed by powers to which

even examiners must bow, and then the answers were in every way satisfactory. 'Shakespeare got most of his materials from Plato,' or 'from Aristotle and Plato,' or 'from De Cameron's *Boccaccio*,' or 'from Collier and Malone.' Excellent children, who refused to be interested in chips from Shakespeare's workshop! So much, then, for what examiners mean by the understanding a play.

Before leaving Shakespeare a word may be added on the selection of plays. Except for the highest examinations *Hamlet* should be proscribed. If a play is to be appreciated by young people, it is of the first importance that the motives of the principal characters should be within their comprehension. Now *Hamlet* lies wholly out of a child's world. The only possible feeling they could entertain for him would be one of contempt, but then this is not what Shakespeare means. I had opportunity of realizing this the present year, when the play was set for the Oxford Junior Local Examination. The general impression among the candidates seemed to be that it was all a very stupid business together, but that in those remote times little else was to be expected.

The authors usually read in school besides Shakespeare are Chaucer, Spenser, and Milton among poets, and in prose Bacon and Burke. Chaucer and Spenser stand together in two respects—first, that they require more glossary work, and secondly, that the poems are more marked by the characteristics

of a particular age, and so require for their comprehension some acquaintance with the ideas of the
time. Chaucer is unintelligible without some clear
notion of the religious and chivalrous ideas of the
fourteenth century, and the *Faery Queene* is unintelligible apart from the Protestant Reformation and the
Italian Renascence. It would be well for teachers
to arrange the period of English history that the
class is studying to correspond with the literature.
To any one who has not experience of the great
ignorance of children, their misapprehensions must
sound incredible. A simple instance is Chaucer's
Squire, who is a great stumbling-block in the badly-
taught schools, the ordinary associations of the word
'squire' being those of present day country gentle-
men—Chaucer's 'Franklin.' Again, the romantic use
of classical mythology, as in the *Knight's Tale*, is
excessively puzzling, and requires careful explanation.
It is often said in examinations that among the prac-
tices of chivalry was a worship of heathen deities.
The teacher will get some help from a book by
Mr. John Saunders on the *Canterbury Tales*. Older
students, such as present themselves for the Joint
Board certificate and offer the *Prologue* and several
of the *Tales*, should study the life of Chaucer, with
its stages of French and Italian influence. Mr.
Pollard's primer of Chaucer is an excellent handbook.
It is worth while also to master the very simple rules
for sounding the final -*e*, upon which the scansion
largely depends. Chaucer was a very exact metrician,

and of course the beauty of his lines must disappear if their rhythm is not understood. Spenser is less confusing to the young than Chaucer, because the sixteenth century lies nearer than the fourteenth, and its history is better known. Dean Kitchin's editions of the first two books give a good idea of the sort of help pupils require. Milton is found difficult for quite another reason. It was said by Mark Pattison that an appreciation of Milton was 'the last reward of consummated scholarship'; without some scholarship he cannot be understood at all. For words are used in classical senses, or with classical associations, and without comprehension of these the sense must be missed. But to Latinists, and in these days girls as well as boys are Latinists, there is no English author the study of whose text so well supplies the sort of intellectual training we have long associated with a study of the classics. I should say that a successful paraphrase of a passage in *Paradise Lost* is the last reward of consummated English scholarship. Such a paraphrase is difficult for two reasons : first, because of the wealth of allusion already referred to, and secondly, from the lines being so closely written. The first difficulty needs no illustration, and teachers are fully alive to it. The second does not meet with enough attention. A good example is afforded by the familiar passage :—

> 'Fall'n cherub, to be weak is miserable
> Doing or suffering ; but of this be sure,
> To do aught good never will be our task.'

The *but* is the key to the position ; any paraphrase that does not bring out the force of this conjunction is useless. The sort of paraphrase the examiner wants would run something as follows : 'It is indeed miserable to find ourselves weaker than the Almighty, whether it obliges us to execute his commands or merely suffer his torments ; but our task (if, as you say, he is to be our task-master) shall not be to do good. So much at least lies in our own will.'

Of the prose books little need be said, for they are not imaginative literature, and so the examination has to be chiefly upon the historical or moral matters discussed. But a few remarks may be in place. Young people should not be set to read Bacon's *Essays*, for the same reason that they should not be set to read *Hamlet* ; and for the further reason that the allusiveness of Bacon's manner will make the study little more than cram. Even for senior pupils only a selection of the *Essays* should be set. Burke is a far more suitable author. But among his speeches it would be well to restrict pupils to those where he has the best of the argument, e. g. the speeches on America. The *French Revolution* is so much a party pamphlet that the pupil has the double labour of learning what Burke has to say, and why he is wrong in saying it. And it is always bad policy to shake a schoolboy's faith in the author to whom his attention is being invited. It might be well, perhaps, to combine with these prose-books one which would be of service to the pupil in the matter of composition.

Candidates for the Joint Board certificate are required to write an essay upon a set subject, and it would assist this purpose if the required amount of Burke or Bacon were reduced and some essays of Goldsmith or Addison put in place.

The chief fault in youthful essays is a declamatory style. It is the debating society that first gives shape and expression to the young idea, and it is natural to young people to hold their ideas with fervour and express them vigorously. Still, an essay is an essay and not a declamation; and the effort to express ideas simply and adequately is all the more salutary that it is so difficult. It would be well for the teacher to issue a Draconian law against all rhetorical particles, and against the rhetorical question in any of its forms. A sentence beginning 'Shall we not love the structure they reared at such a cost, the magnificent structure —— ' &c., or 'What of William Pitt and William of Orange, Dupleix and Hannibal?' &c., should be scored out, however sonorous. At the other pole, but equally to be condemned, are those essays which button-hole the examiner, and are full of colloquialisms, especially the colloquial use of ' *one*,' as in 'one goes on one's way.' The first advice an examiner would give to the writer of school essays is to write upon the subject. No doubt some of the most charming English essays are amongst the most rambling. But a 'theme,' to use the old term, should keep to the point. One essay sent in this year on 'A Country Walk in Spring' was for the most part a diatribe against the alleged gluttony of the monastic orders, a connecting link being found in the ruins of Bolton Abbey, which presented themselves in the course of the walk. Another hint would be to make first of all a rough sketch of the plan to be pursued, so that if excursions are made, there may yet be a way of return.

I have been much struck with the very great difference between school and school in this matter of essay-writing. In some schools even the best pupils cannot write two pages upon a simple subject, on which they cannot fail to have ideas; in others the essays sent in are fluent and thoroughly well written. Composition therefore can be taught. It is probably best taught, as it is taught usually, by translation from and into Latin and Greek; but on modern sides and in girls' schools, where the classical training is not so thorough, English composition should receive proportionately more careful study. Younger students will find in Dr. Abbott's *How to Write Clearly* useful rules for avoiding the most common pitfalls; for older students nothing can supersede a diligent study of good models under a good teacher. It might be found useful occasionally to supply heads for an essay to be written in school, so that the treatment and composition might receive all the attention, and by a comparison of essays the more backward pupils learn from the best.

H. C. BEECHING.

THE MATRICULATION EXAMINATION
OF THE UNIVERSITY OF LONDON

OF all the Public Examinations there is probably none that is so popular, to use the word in its strict sense, as the Matriculation Examination of London University. The number of candidates of both sexes appears to be largely and steadily on the increase, and there is no other examination which in any way competes with it on its own ground.

The reasons for its popularity are obvious. In the first place a London B.A. or M.A. degree has gradually become more and more valuable in the estimation of the public. It is well known that, in order to secure such a degree, a wider curriculum is required than for the corresponding Pass degrees at Oxford or Cambridge, and as this has been more generally recognized, we find graduates of London University considered eligible for many posts which not so very long ago were practically closed to all except to graduates of the two older Universities. This has been especially noticeable with regard to head-masterships; and many head-masters, moreover, seem to think that, as far as teaching is concerned, the London University course is more conducive to thoroughness than that of either Oxford or Cambridge.

So pronounced is the feeling of the public generally with regard to the stamp imprinted on a man by residence in a College and by the general life of a University, that it is in no way likely that the London B.A. or M.A. will ever be regarded as actually on a par with the Oxford or Cambridge degrees; but there can be no doubt that very considerable pres- tige attaches to any London degree, while a London D.Litt. or D.Sc. would certainly have a distinguished career in any University in the world.

Now the London Matriculation Examination is the entrance to the University career, and it may be taken for granted that any one who can pass the examination has a fair chance of obtaining his B.A. degree. This is by no means the case at Oxford or Cambridge. As we well know, there is no University Matriculation Examination at either of those Universities; each College fixes its own standard, and the difficulty of a College Matricula- tion Examination is usually in inverse ratio to the popularity of the College. At some Colleges the examination is hard and more or less competitive; at some it is a moderate test of ability; but at others it is little more than a form. An appreciable proportion (though, we may hope, a gradually lessening one) of the whole number of undergraduates go up without any idea of taking a degree, and a very large proportion would never enter at all if they

had to pass an examination approaching in any degree
in difficulty to that for the London Matriculation. This
is all very well where residence is enforced, and any
alteration would be much to be deprecated under
present circumstances; but the case is very different
where there is no residence to be kept whatever,
and London University therefore rightly makes its
examination a real test of knowledge.

In the second place the London Matriculation
Examination is the professional examination *par
excellence*. We must not trench on a subject treated
of in another part of this volume, but we may
perhaps go so far as to say that we believe
we are quite in accord with many, if not most,
head-masters in thinking that professional examinations are largely overdone, and that the whole
question will before long require very serious
consideration. Be this, however, as it may, there
is, as far as we know, no profession requiring
a Preliminary Examination which does not accept
the London Matriculation in lieu of that examination, and all who feel that they have a chance of
passing it naturally enter for it, since it gives them at
one and the same time an entrance to their profession
and a chance of a degree in the future.

In the third place the examination is generally
considered to be an excellent test of a good all-round
education, and is therefore adopted by many schools
as a leaving examination for the higher boys. So
important indeed are its advantages that several

of the larger public schools which used to ignore it or to compel boys to work for it out of school hours if they wished to enter for it, have now felt compelled to start a London Matriculation Class, in the same way that in former years they were forced to establish Modern Sides and Army Classes.

As the examination has grown in popularity it has, of course, come in for a large share of criticism, and from time to time radical alterations have been made by the authorities, who have on many occasions shown themselves most willing to listen to the representations of head-masters and other interested teachers with regard to anomalies and possible improvements in the examination. And here it may not be out of place to refer to a few particulars concerning the history of the examination[1]. The first examination appears to have been held in the year 1838. Twenty-three candidates were examined and twenty-two passed, the average age being just eighteen. There were in fact three separate examinations, a Pass Examination commencing November 5, an Examination for Honours in Mathematics and Natural Philosophy, commencing November 13, and an Examination for Honours in Classics,

[1] For these and for the statistics given on p. 236, and for much help in the papers, the writer is greatly indebted to Mr. R. W. Hinton, of the Haberdashers' School, Hoxton, who has served for some time on the Annual Committee of the London University, and on various sub-committees, and has therefore had access to the older Calendars and to the Proceedings.

commencing November 20. The papers for the Pass Examination comprised Arithmetic and Algebra, English History (apparently as far as the end of the Stuart Period), Outlines of Ancient and Modern Geography, Greek Classic and History, Chemistry, Natural History (Botany and Zoology), Algebra and Geometry, and Roman Classic and History. The papers were set in the order above mentioned. It will be seen that the examination differed very widely from what it is at present; one of the chief features was the great length of the classical papers. Examiners are more careful of themselves nowadays. The candidates who passed in the first examination went in again for Honours, and five out of eight obtained Honours in both Classics and Mathematics.

The following table will show the growth of the examination up to the present time :—

Year.	Number Examined.	Number Passed.	Percentage of Passes.	Average Age Yrs. Mths.	
1838	23	22	95·65	17	11
1840	77	69	89·61	19	6
1845	113	103	91·15	19	6
1850	206	190	92·23	19	3
1855	209	172	82·29	19	5
1860	428	291	67·99	19	11
1865	616	397	64·44	20	8
1870	828	420	50·72	19	11
1875	1016	542	53·34	19	9
1880	1400 [1]	848	60·57	19	9
1885	1900	1094	57·57	not given	
1890	2762	1278	46·27	,,	
1895	3420	1710	50		
1896	3327	1566	47·06		
1897	3416	1698	48·38		

[1] In 1879 the Matriculation Examination was opened to

The last entry is as large as any yet made, and the growth is very striking, especially when we remember that in 1847 the examiners complained of deficient accommodation, as there were 160 candidates.

In 1845, which is the earliest year for which a Calendar was obtainable, we find that the examination was held once a year, beginning on the first Monday in July; the age was to be certified as over sixteen, and the fee was fixed at £2. The syllabus was as follows for a Pass, the Honours Examinations being separate :—

1. *Mathematics*: *Arithmetic*, as now; *Algebra*, to simple equations only; *Geometry*, *Euclid*, Book I. The questions were all very elementary.

2. *Natural Philosophy*, much as it has been up to the present time, but alternative to *Chemistry*, which was a wider subject than at present.

3. *Classics*: Xenophon, *Memorabilia II*, and Virgil, *Georgic IV*.

4. *English*, including History and Geography. The questions would appear somewhat quaint nowadays. Proficiency in composition was to be judged by the general style of a candidate's answers.

At the institution of the examination in 1838 only collegiate students were admissible, and of the

women, and the previously existing General Examination for Women was abolished.

twenty-two who passed, thirteen came from University College and nine from King's College.   In 1839 Mr. Warburton carried his motion : 'to omit from the certificate to be produced before Matriculation the words, "and that he has been admitted as a student at one of the institutions in connexion with this University."'   This really laid the foundation of the examination as at present existing.   The concession was apparently not much appreciated at first, for in 1841 we find only three outsiders among those who passed ; in 1850, however, the number had risen to thirty-five out of one hundred and ninety, and since that time has steadily increased.

In 1853 Natural Philosophy and Chemistry were both made obligatory, and French, with the alternative of German, was added in the form of translations from set books.   When we remember that under the new regulations, which will come into force in 1899, one language only, besides English (viz. Latin), is compulsory, it will be seen how radical has been the change since the years in which no candidate could pass without three.

In 1857 a great change was made in the constitution of the University.   A new draft charter was prepared, under which it was proposed to abolish the rule restricting degrees to those who had passed two years in an Affiliated College.   A great battle ensued, the Colleges being all strongly opposed, with the exception of King's, which held aloof ; but by the exertions of Sir R. Quain, Sir R. Barnes, and

Dr. Todhunter the clause was carried, and became law in April, 1858, to the great benefit of education generally. Indirectly of course this had an important bearing on the future of the Matriculation Examination.

One of the great objections always raised against the examination is that it embraces too wide a range of subjects, and that, to be successful, a candidate must pass in Classics, Mathematics, and Science. All persons who have had anything to do with the preparation for the examination must have felt the force of this. There are usually some boys in every school who are good all round, but there are always a considerable number who are one-sided, and who cannot master sufficient Mathematics to pass; these have necessarily been excluded, although their subsequent career may have been much more brilliant than that of the others. Of course we have the crucial example of this state of things in the old custom at Cambridge of making the Mathematical Tripos compulsory. In the latter case, however, the mathematical men at least were satisfied, but in the case of the Matriculation Examination no one is satisfied, as the mathematical candidates complain that there is too much 'Arts,' and the 'Arts' candidates that there is too much Mathematics and Science. In the face of the objection, however, it is interesting to note that in 1861 it was stated as the *avowed object* of the Matriculation Examination 'to encourage a good grounding in a considerable number of subjects rather than proficiency in a few,' and on this ground certain radical alterations were made, the chief being the discontinuance of the separate Honours Examination and the fixing of a maximum of marks for each of the three divisions of the examination, which remain the same to the present day.

Apparently, however, it was 'advanced proficiency' rather than 'good grounding' which the examiners aimed at; for the examination appears to have increased in difficulty, until in 1870 the Examinations Committee received a Resolution from Convocation to the effect 'that it is desirable that the Senate should consider the propriety of lessening the difficulty of the Matriculation Examination.' Convocation alleged three reasons for their action: firstly, the increased proportion of failures (nearly 50 per cent.); secondly, the general rise of the standard, as proved by more difficult questions and more severe marking; and thirdly, the fact that the best Colleges and Schools complained of the severity of the examination. The Examinations Committee of the Senate replied in detail, and practically promised to be more lenient. Moreover, in 1874 the Senate allowed German as an alternative to Greek, and in 1877 instructed the examiners to allow a candidate to pass in Geometry 'who has honestly studied the text of the first four books' of Euclid. Matters, however, went on apparently much as before, until in January, 1882, a climax was reached, only 298 candidates passing out of 736, and only ten of these being in the Honours Division.

The Senate directed the attention of the examiners to this, and passed the following resolution, which ought to be impressed, in its main points, upon all examiners in a similar position : ' That it be an instruction to the Registrar to inform all examiners on their appointment that the Matriculation Examination is primarily intended for students of sixteen or seventeen years of age, and to remind them that the papers in each subject form a part only of the formidable ordeal of an examination lasting for five days; therefore, that while the knowledge required of each subject should be sound as far as it goes, the examination should never be otherwise than of a simple elementary character, within the limits of the syllabus, more searching tests being reserved for later examinations.'

It would take much more space than we have at our disposal to give an account of the proceedings of Convocation with regard to the Matriculation Examination during the past fifteen years. The greatest credit, however, is due to the authorities for the efforts they have made, on nearly all occasions, to meet the views of their critics and to render the examination as useful as possible to candidates of varying types. If they appear to have failed in some points, it is not due to neglect or want of will, but to the circumstances of the case, the examination having grown to such an extent that it has been perfectly impossible to please everybody.

It is evident that the shortcomings of the examina-

R

tion have been at times strongly felt, for the sub-committee appointed by the Annual Committee, December 5, 1884, commence their Report with the following words : 'Considerable dissatisfaction with the Matriculation Examination having been expressed in more than one influential quarter, it was thought advisable not to disregard opinions proceeding from acknowledged friends of education.' The sub-committee on their part, before issuing the Report, had certainly done their best to find out the opinions of the head-masters of the chief schools, by sending round a circular letter containing various questions calculated to bring out their views as to the arrangement and subjects of the examination. In the large number of answers received there was on some points, as for instance the retention of Latin as compulsory, a definite consensus, while on others there was a very considerable divergence of opinion. The Senate gave the fullest consideration to all the points submitted by Convocation, and the result was practically the syllabus in vogue at the present time, which is as follows :—

1. Latin.
2. *One* of the following languages : Greek, French, German, Sanskrit, Arabic.
3. The English Language ; and English History, with the Geography relating thereto.
4. Mathematics.
5. Mechanics.

6. *One* of the following branches of Science:
Chemistry; Heat and Light; Magnetism
and Electricity; Botany.

In the original Report of the sub-committee
two languages were recommended besides Latin;
and no mention was made of either Geography or
Botany.

We have seen how the question of the increasing
difficulty of the examination has been carefully considered from time to time by the authorities, but
a much more fruitful source of discontent was for
a long time perhaps more or less unconsciously
ignored, and cannot yet be said to have been fully
dealt with. This is the great variability of the
standard of the papers. The *Journal of Education*
some time ago published a series of curves showing
the variation of results from year to year. This
variation is evidently not dependent on any great
difference in the capacity of teachers or candidates,
for where so large a number of candidates present
themselves any occasional wide divergence from a
normal standard is corrected by the law of averages.
From letters received from well-known head-masters,
and from personal experience, we can testify that
this has been the chief objection brought against
the examination. There seems to be a belief that
matters are now much improved, but there appears
to be no definite Revising Committee, such as is
appointed by the delegates of several other Public

Examinations; at any rate, there is none that acts uniformly and systematically[1].

The variability has not been confined to the Matriculation Examination, for in 1889 we find a sub-committee appointed by Convocation to consider the matter in view of the fact 'that of thirty-nine candidates in Mixed Mathematics for the B.A. Examination in 1884, none failed, and of sixty-nine candidates in 1888, forty-seven failed, showing a proportion of failure very largely in excess of that in any other subject.'

Another point that might well be considered is the feasibility of altering the present dates of the examination, viz. January and June. These times are most inconvenient for schools, and it is from schools that the chief number of Matriculation candidates are derived. We believe that it is stated that the arrangements for other examinations preclude the authorities from complying with any request to alter the dates, but it would appear that the question of any particular time is of less importance for candidates for the higher degrees than for those presenting themselves for Matriculation, and that therefore the possibility of the alteration of the

[1] From a past examiner we gathered that there was such a body, but that it was practically ineffective; since writing the above, however, we have been informed on good authority that 'there is *no* Revising Committee; the two examiners in each subject are nominally responsible, jointly and severally, but the results show that the obligation is not sufficiently stringent.'

present dates might well be taken into consideration, to the advantage of a large number of those who send in candidates, as well as of the candidates themselves.

We have purposely refrained from any criticism of the present syllabus, because it will expire in 1899, when the new regulations, which have recently been published, will come into force. It was known that certain alterations were contemplated, but the changes to be introduced are more radical than were expected, and have, we think, been somewhat prematurely sprung upon us, without such previous consultation with experienced teachers as might easily have been secured by a circular letter.

The new syllabus is as follows :—

1. Latin (two papers).
2. English (two papers).
3. Mathematics (two papers).
4. General Elementary Science (two papers).
5. Any one of the following Languages or Sciences :—Greek, French, German, Sanskrit, Arabic ; Elementary Mechanics, Elementary Chemistry, Elementary Sound Heat and Light, Elementary Magnetism and Electricity, Elementary Botany (one paper).

The time allowed to Latin is extended from four to six hours. This is an improvement, but, on the other hand, the small catchy sentences for translation from English into Latin (somewhat humorously described as 'simple and easy') appear to be retained, in the face of strong representations that a piece of 'easy consecutive prose' would be far preferable.

In English stress is no longer laid upon the 'general history and grammatical structure of the language'; it now becomes 'English Grammar and Composition, with elementary questions on the history of the language and literature,' which is certainly an improvement.

The subject of Mathematics remains the same; but Mechanics is dropped as a compulsory subject, and great changes are introduced in the Science, two papers on General Elementary Science taking the place of the single Mechanics paper. We have no space to discuss the General Science syllabus, but at first sight it strikes us as much too eclectic and discursive, and it seems very probable, to judge by past experience, that, unless great care is taken in setting and revising the papers, it will be found that while the Mechanics scourged us with whips, the General Elementary Science will scourge us with scorpions. At the same time the idea is a good one, and we agree with the editor of *Education* (September 11, 1897), 'that the notion of making an Elementary School Course in Physics, Mechanics, and Chemistry the basis of all scientific study has already been widely accepted,' and that the present arrangement will naturally lead candidates to specialize for the branch of science which is most attractive to them.

But we are further of opinion that the same writer puts his finger on the great blot of the whole syllabus when he takes exception to the inevitable decline and probable disappearance of French, and the consequent disorganization of school curricula. As the candidate *must* have his grounding in General Elementary Science, and as the term 'elementary' is applied separately to every science mentioned under Section 5, it is evident that a majority of candidates will take up one of these sciences as their Optional Subject. French will therefore be dropped, and, it is to be feared, will too often be entirely neglected, a result very greatly to be deprecated in these days of foreign competition.

There are one or two other points which have been considered by the Incorporated Association of Head-masters, and which we confess we should like to have seen altered, but it is hardly worth while to discuss them in the face of the new syllabus.

One matter however we may perhaps be allowed briefly to touch upon, in conclusion, although it is a somewhat delicate one. An examination on a scale so vast as the London Matriculation Examination, and carrying such important results, might naturally be expected to give rise to a system of special tuition, which is usually designated by the word 'cram'; and, as a matter of fact, we find the system reduced almost to a fine art with regard to the London University Examinations. It is not for us here to criticize the system as such; the names of those engaged in the work stand deservedly high, and the text-books issued by them (though in the case of classical authors much too exhaustive and tending to put a premium upon indolence) are in their way excellent; but the very knowledge that such a system exists tends to disgust examiners, and tempts them to invent catchy questions, which fall indeed within the strict syllabus, but are scarcely fair to ordinary candidates. This is sometimes very noticeable in the mathematical papers.

In spite however of all criticism, in the face of all objections, the fact remains that the popularity of the examination (as evinced by the number of candidates) is steadily increasing. This, of itself, is a proof of its real worth and of the care with which it is on the whole conducted. At the same time it is becoming an ever-increasing responsibility, and we may perhaps be allowed to express a hope that the authorities will meet that responsibility in the future as in the past, and that they will, to this end, allow those outsiders who are most interested in the examination as much voice in prospective changes as their predecessors have done during the past fifty years.

W. W. FOWLER.

' Indeed, if this good man had an enthusiasm, or what the vulgar call a blind side, it was this—he thought a schoolmaster the greatest character in the world, and himself the greatest of all schoolmasters ; neither of which points he would have given up to Alexander the Great at the head of his army.'—FIELDING, on Parson Adams.

' He was, indeed, deeply imbued with that fortunate vanity which alone could induce a man who has arms to pare and burn a muir to submit to the yet more toilsome task of cultivating youth.'—SIR W. SCOTT, on the Rector of Edinburgh High School.

THESE quotations, from two writers who are usually wise and just and always manly, illustrate very well the attitude of amused contempt with which the robust Briton has always regarded the scholastic profession. No doubt a man who, by combining the offices of schoolmaster, priest, and keeper of a boarding-house, makes several thousand pounds a year, can be sure of the respect of all persons of right feeling and inferior income ; but everybody is aware that a schoolmaster, so long as he remains a schoolmaster only, cannot aspire either to large earnings or to any public distinctions ; and it is natural to conclude that no one would adopt a profession so arduous and yet so mean, without some grave defects in his mental and moral constitution. This opinion seems indeed to be peculiar to the inhabitants of this island, but I am not now concerned to refute it. My business in this article is merely to show, by a particular instance, that the antagonism between the public and the schoolmasters, which exists only here, has led to grave inconveniences of a kind which also exists only here. On the one hand, schoolmasters, even the best qualified, seeing themselves despised, have not combined to assert their dignity, as the doctors and lawyers do, but have taken refuge most unnecessarily in the clerical profession and have neglected that by which they make their bread. On the other hand, the public have allowed all manner of persons to set up for schoolmasters, and all manner of other persons to prescribe the subjects and standards of learning. At a time when it is thought that our educational system will be perfected by creating a second set of school boards in every town and county, it will be especially useful to consider how many authorities already exist, which, though they have no direct control over the schools, can yet put an iron compulsion on the scholars and defy any merely local efforts at reform.

The absurd perplexities of our elementary schools do not fall within the scope of this article, but I cannot refrain from observing that, on the intellectual side, elementary education seems to me far more chaotic than secondary. Apart from reading, writing and arithmetic, which are not now taught very strenuously, our Code, the much-vaunted Code, which is made in a government office, of course without the assistance of schoolmasters, provides at least seven hundred and twenty different curricula of four subjects each. Each of these may be further complicated by a selection from the subjects, over twenty in number, recommended by the Science and Art Department. How many curricula are actually in use nobody knows, but the number is certainly enormous. What system of technical education can be built on such a shifting foundation? Here is a point at which the secondary school board will soon find itself utterly frustrated by the primary.

Sed haec hactenus: let me return to my proper subject, the secondary schools, and observe, as I do with a certain malicious pleasure, the grave public inconvenience which, as I have said, arises from the public neglect and contempt of the scholastic profession. In the first place, it is to be remarked that the curricula of secondary schools, that is to say, the choice of subjects, the order in which they are taught, the methods of teaching and the standards to be attained, are all practically in the control of the head-master or proprietor. Occasional checks there are, in the shape of schemes of the Charity Commission and Boards of Governors, but generally a head-master, if he cannot get his own way by hook, can manage to get it by crook.   In my opinion this is a bad thing for the profession, because it prevents the discussion of that which is the main business of the profession.   Schoolmasters, when they meet in council, discuss anything rather than curricula or methods of teaching, simply because on these matters every man is a law to himself, and, if we have some ideals in common, they are ideals made, not by ourselves, but by some external body of examiners.   But this autocracy of head-masters, though it is bad for the profession, need not be so bad for the public ; since, if a parent cannot educate his sons for himself, surely it is not unwise to entrust their education to a man who is himself highly educated, who is a practised teacher, and who is bound, by the nature of his work, to lead an ascetic and honourable life.   It is at least not an uncommon nor an unfounded opinion that the main objects of education were better secured fifty years ago, when education was frankly left to the school-master, as physicking to the doctor.   But unfortunately the contempt for schoolmasters, which was always latent, has recently become very active. Nobody nowadays will take a schoolmaster's word, as he takes the word of a doctor however stupid. There must be an examination to find out whether what the schoolmaster says is true, and whether a boy is really fit, after all his schooling, to enter civilized society.   Then, when one corporate body sets up an examination, every other must needs set up a different one, to show its independence. The result is that the approach to every University and every profession is now blocked by an examination, devised and conducted by unknown and irresponsible and perhaps incompetent persons, who are nevertheless very precise and insistent in their requirements, and there are so many examinations that no school, even a very large one, can possibly prepare for them all, or even prepare for two or three only, without grave injury to its proper work of education.

It may be left to reactionaries to discuss whether examinations really serve any useful purpose which was not effectually served before. For my part, I am very willing to concede that examinations have their uses, and I am contending only that they should be few and well-designed, and that, as it is, a grave public nuisance is caused by their number and diversity. Who can say how many compulsory preliminary examinations there are, not intended at all to discover merit, but merely to exclude gross ignorance and stupidity? I am speaking, of course, only of examinations which are designed for school-boys, and are intended to be passed by candidates on leaving school. Of such examinations the following list, though it is surprisingly long, is probably not exhaustive. The five English Universities, Oxford, Cambridge, London, Durham, and Victoria, have each a separate entrance examination, which for shortness, strict accuracy not being required for the moment, I will call matriculation. There are separate examinations for entrance into the various training colleges of the Army and Navy, and, though examinations for the Civil Service stand on a different footing (since here examination leads directly to paid employment\, yet the number and diversity of these examinations causes great and unnecessary hardship.　Lastly, an entrance examination is required by the following incorporated professions : Barristers, Solicitors, Doctors, Dentists, Veterinary Surgeons, Civil Engineers, Architects, Actuaries, Chartered Accountants, Society of Accountants, Pharmaceutical Chemists.　With only a few exceptions, the examination which suffices to admit a boy to one of these Universities or Colleges or professions will not suffice to admit him to any other.　The main exceptions are these : Oxford and Cambridge have devised a joint examination of schools, granting a certificate which will in some cases admit to either University, and the doctors, dentists and veterinary surgeons have agreed to a common scheme for their preliminary examinations.　As a rule, every profession insists stoutly upon its own definition of adequate education, and though it does not insist on granting its own certificate, yet it does require that the certificate shall have been granted by some important body of examiners and shall contain every item of the definition.　For instance, I have recently seen two cases in which boys who wished to be articled as accountants presented certificates in Honours of the Cambridge Local Examination, but were rejected because the certificates did not contain geography. Similarly, though London matriculation is now accepted by all the professions, yet when it is possible, as it soon will be, to pass it with no other foreign language but Latin, the General Medical Council, which requires one other foreign language in its preliminary examination, will doubtless reject matriculation certificates which do not contain two languages.

I suppose that all these examinations are intended for the average boy, but there is a bewildering diversity in the subjects and standards set. Thus, to take an extreme instance, the Civil Service Commission offers employment to boy-clerks, aged from fifteen to seventeen, on the results of an examination in Handwriting, Orthography, Arithmetic (including Vulgar and Decimal Fractions), Copying MS. (to test accuracy), English Composition, Geography. But the London Chamber of Commerce, without offering any employment at all, expects a boy of the same age to pass an examination in (1) English (including Handwriting, Orthography, Grammar, and Composition), (2) Commercial History of the British Isles, Colonies and Dependencies, Geography, including the elements of Physical Geography, and ordinary Geography, with special reference to commerce and industry ; (3) Arithmetic, including a general knowledge of Foreign Weights and Measures, Currencies and Exchanges ; (4) Mathematics, including Algebra to Quadratic Equations, Euclid I–III,

and Mechanics; (5) Book-keeping and Accounts;
(6) a Modern Foreign Language, comprising translation, composition, dictation, and conversation;
(7) Elementary Drawing; (8) one at least of seven
optional subjects (in which Latin is not included).
It is obvious that a boy who devotes the necessary
time for either of these examinations is *ipso Yacto*
debarring himself from every other career, for he will
drop Latin, and Latin is required for almost every
other preliminary examination. Suppose, however,
that in order to preserve his liberty, he keeps up
his Latin. He will now find that there are remarkable divergences in the requirements of the
various professional corporations. Thus the Society
of Accountants requires only Algebra to Fractions
and Euclid I, while the Institute of Chartered Accountants requires Algebra to Quadratics and Euclid
I–IV.   The Institute of Actuaries requires only
Algebra to Simple Equations and no Euclid at all.
The Incorporated Law Society requires (if mathematics are taken) Algebra to Simple Equations and
Euclid I–IV.   The Institute of Civil Engineers
requires Algebra to the Binomial Theorem, Loga-
rithms, Trigonometry to the solution of triangles,
Euclid I–IV, Projective Geometry, and Elementary
Analytical Geometry. Suppose, again, that a boy,
determined to be free of all the professions, passes
the Cambridge Senior Local Examination in all the
subjects that any professional corporation requires.
He is still excluded from the services and from every

University, for even Cambridge will not allow him to read for a degree unless he passes in Divinity and Greek along with other elementary subjects. Nor is it to be assumed that a boy who passes one examination can quickly pass another of nearly the same standard ; for most of these examinations have different set books, set periods of history, and so forth, and the knowledge which was serviceable once will not all be serviceable again. Moreover, in all public examinations, even the Locals, no certificate is given unless the candidate passes in the proposed minimum of subjects, so that, if he fails by a bare margin, his work is not recognized *quantum valeat.* For instance, it would be feasible enough to give a boy, who failed for the Joint Board Certificate or in the Army Examination, a statement of the subjects in which he passed, which statement might suffice to free him from some professional examinations. But for the most part there is no such practice. If a candidate fails in the examination of his first choice, he must begin *de novo* for this and every other examination.

It should be remembered that no school is bound to prepare pupils for any public examination, and that certainly some schools, and those not the worst, take no notice of external examinations at all. But, with the best will in the world to serve the public convenience, no school can possibly prepare for all the examinations above enumerated, and very few can prepare for more than two or three. I can imagine a very large and wealthy school which should prepare its pupils for the Cambridge Local at Christmas and the Joint Board Examination in July, and should also have special classes for the Army, the Navy, the Civil Service, and for London matriculation ; but no existing school does so much as this.   Moreover, even if a school prepares for a Local examination, it is impossible so to conduct a large class as to make sure that each boy shall pass in every subject demanded as a preliminary to his chosen profession.   The consequence is that many boys, after a long and expensive education at school, are unable to enter a profession or University without resorting to a crammer ; and if, having made a wrong choice at first, or for any other reason, a boy or man desires to change his profession, he may very likely have to begin again and study for a new preliminary examination.   Such is the annoyance and expense to which the public is exposed, and not unjustly exposed, as a punishment for its persistent neglect of the intellectual side of secondary education.   It has never called upon the experts for any theory, and the experts have not thought it necessary to agree upon one.   The University of Oxford has its own opinion upon the proper subjects of instruction at schools ; the University of London has another and a very different one ; the Engineers have another, the Pharmaceutical Chemists another, the Civil Service Commission has about sixty, and every schoolmaster has, or may if he likes, have his own ; and none of these authorities will yield to any other. We were told, at the Cambridge Conference, to maintain at all hazards the present admirable 'liberty, variety, and elasticity' of our secondary education. I see the liberty and variety very plainly, but where is the elasticity?

The ideal remedy for this state of things would, in my judgment, be secured if a competent and permanent educational council, not wholly of school-masters, were appointed, with power to draw up a series of typical curricula for secondary schools, such curricula being divided into standards suitable for the First Form, Second Form, and so on. Each school should then be required (1) to adopt its type or types (for a large school might well adopt two or three types at once); (2) to publish full statistics of its work ; and (3) to submit to occasional inspection in order to guarantee that its professed standards are really maintained. It would then be open to any University or profession to say, 'We will not take boys from schools of such or such a type, or from any form below the nth.' Boys who reached the required form in a school of the recognized type should be admitted to their chosen career on the schoolmaster's certificate, without further examination ; but public examinations corresponding to each of the higher standards should be instituted in order to enable boys, who had attended the wrong school or had failed to reach the required standard, to retrieve their position. Such examinations would be

a public convenience, and not a public nuisance.
I am persuaded that by this arrangement the Universities and the professions would have no grievance, while the schools and the public would gain certain enormous advantages. It would be a good thing for schoolmasters to exclude charlatans from the profession, to be placed in a position of definite trust, to be expected to meet a simple set of requirements, to discuss with one another how best to meet such requirements, to aspire to the honour of a seat on an educational council, and so forth. It would be a good thing for the public to be relieved of examinations which waste time that might be spent in learning, to understand what goes on in the schools, to know what standard an average boy ought to reach at a given age, to be assured that, if a boy must be transferred from one school to another, he will not suffer much by the change, to perceive a certain definite advantage in leaving a boy at school for one standard more, and so forth. Many other benefits could be named which would result from this plan. If however the public is so distrustful of schoolmasters that it will not dispense with examinations, at least let there be some compromise. Let there be, for instance, three public examinations of different types and standards, such that a boy who passes the highest examination shall be free to go anywhere and do anything. If such examinations were instituted, the schools would soon fall into types accordingly ; but the main objection to

this scheme is that uniformity produced by examinations is bound to have some bad effects on schools and schoolmasters. It is not a good thing to be thinking how to dodge the examiners, to omit this subject because it is never set, to lay stress on that because it is often set, to neglect the clever boy because he is safe, and cram the dull boy because he is doubtful. That is what is done now, with the result that few boys will learn more than is required for their examination, and still fewer will learn anything at all when their examinations are over. To receive a public certificate that he knows enough is debasing to anybody's brains.

J. Gow.

MATRICULATION, RESPONSIONS, AND THE HIGHER CERTIFICATE EXAMINATION

THE school boy coming to the University has two barriers to pass: (1) he has to satisfy the requirements of a College by passing what is still called a 'Matriculation Examination,' though 'entrance examination' would be the better name; (2) he has to pass the first University Examination before he can settle down to what are properly University studies. In the old days it was only possible for Oxford men to take 'Smalls' after they came up; now many Colleges require a man to pass before residing, and as a matter of fact by far the larger proportion of undergraduates, by passing this or an equivalent examination before they reside, are able when they come up to begin their University studies at once. Roughly speaking, the situation is this:—

1. Most Colleges require a man to pass 'Smalls' or its equivalent before residing.

2. Some Colleges accept 'Smalls' or a Certificate as equivalent to an entrance examination; others

expect their men to take some at least of the papers in the College examination (e. g. the General English paper) before they are admitted [1].

From this it appears that Responsions, the Matriculation Examinations of the Colleges, and the Examination for Higher Certificates, are very closely connected. They all, in so far as they command the entrance to the Universities, help to set the standard for the higher Forms of secondary schools. My concern is mainly with the Certificate Examination, but it will be convenient to say first a few words about its relation to the other two examinations.

1. One or more Higher Certificates which include Latin, Greek, and Elementary Mathematics exempt a boy from Responsions; distinction in Latin or Greek or a Pass in French or German exempt him from the Additional Subject.

2. He may also obtain exemption from Responsions if (without obtaining a Higher Certificate of the Board) he satisfies the examiners of the Board in the exact equivalent of Responsions, i. e. Latin Grammar, Prose and Book; Greek Grammar and Book; Arithmetic and either Euclid I, II, or Algebra.

---

[1] What is said throughout this essay of Responsions at Oxford may be understood to apply *mutatis mutandis* to the Previous Examination at Cambridge. It is convenient to speak chiefly of Responsions, as its relation to the Higher Certificate Examination is simpler. The conditions of exemption from the various parts of the Previous Examination are given below.

The exemptions from the Previous Examination are of a similar kind. The conditions are as follows :—

1. Certificates exempt from the First Part of the Previous Examination when they state that the candidate has passed in Scripture Knowledge (showing a satisfactory acquaintance with the Greek Text), Greek, and Latin ; (2) from the Second Part when the candidate has passed in Scripture Knowledge, Elementary and Additional Mathematics, and English or English Prose Composition ; (3) and from the Examination in the Additional Subjects when the candidate has passed in either Trigonometry, Statics, and Dynamics, or in French or in German.

2. A candidate for a certificate—although he does not gain a certificate—may be specially exempted from the various parts of the Previous Examination in the following ways :—

From Part I, if he has satisfied the examiners appointed by the Board at one and the same examination in one Greek Book (or Unprepared Greek Translation), in one Latin Book (or Latin Prose Composition), in Greek and Latin Grammar, in Unprepared Latin Translation, and in a Prepared Book of the Old or New Testament, showing a satisfactory knowledge of the Greek Text.

From Part II (except the English Essay), if he has satisfied the examiners appointed by the Board at one and the same examination in the paper on the Four Gospels, together with the outlines of the history contained in the Old Testament, in Elementary Mathematics and in Algebra and Euclid, as required for passing in Additional Mathematics; and further from the English Essay, if he has satisfied the examiners in English or English Prose Composition.

From the Additional Subjects, if he has satisfied the examiners appointed by the Board in either Trigonometry, Statics and Dynamics at one and the same examination, or in French or in German.

Boys who hold a certificate or group of certificates of this sort would be accepted at most Colleges in both Universities with little or no further examination, provided that other conditions were satisfied.

From this it appears that the certificate, as things are, represents pretty fairly the standard that is to be aimed at by a public school boy who intends to go to an 'Honour College,' and therefore in a volume dealing with school teaching it is natural that this examination should find a place. Since its establishment in 1874, most of the secondary schools of the highest grade, with a few notable exceptions[1], have taken the examination either yearly or once in two or three years. It is therefore worth while to consider the bearings of the examination on public school teaching.

It will be understood that what I say in this paper

---

[1] Charterhouse and Haileybury have stood aloof from the examination; Shrewsbury, Merchant Taylors', and the City of London School are regularly examined by the Joint Board, but do not take the Examination for Certificates.

is not at any point an official utterance of the Board, but my personal view, based upon ten years' experience as one of its Secretaries and on some practical knowledge of teaching in school and college.

The Board, like most English institutions, is the creation of compromise. The public schools, threatened after the Commission of 1867 with Government examination and inspection, turned to the Universities, and the institution of the Oxford and Cambridge Schools Examination Board was the result. The schools consented to give up their old independent and voluntary examinations and to receive instead examiners appointed by a University Board; they gained a *quid pro quo* in the exemption of their pupils under certain conditions from the first University examinations. This, it must be borne in mind, is and was an essential feature in the examination, and the criticisms passed upon it which ignore this relation to University examinations are beside the point. No doubt the schools which have held aloof gain some independence, though it is a question whether they really enjoy more freedom of study; but, on the other hand, they impose an inconvenient burden on their pupils, who cannot get their exemption from the University examination without a journey to Oxford or Cambridge; and it is to be hoped that in the long run they will find it possible to conform to the general practice of the public schools. Three things, it may be safely

asserted, have been achieved by the Board: (1) There
is a better economy in the trained examining ability
of the country than was possible under what may be
called the purely voluntary system; (2) the standard
set by the examiners and their judgment on the
schools examined is less variable and uncertain;
(3) the channel of communication between schools of
the highest grade and the older Universities opened
by the institution of the Joint Board has helped to
promote a better understanding between them and
to adjust their relations. The informal conferences
held from time to time between the committee of
the Head-Masters' Conference and representatives
of the Board have been found very useful for the
discussion and explanation of the policy of the Board
and for the suggestion of changes in the arrangements of its examinations.

Besides bringing the schools into closer communication with the Universities and making them more
acquainted with University standards, the Higher
Certificate Examination has produced very definite
effects on the standard of school teaching in certain
subjects. The average public school boy does much
better in Mathematics than he did twenty years ago;
the average standard of Unprepared Translation
from Latin and Greek is very distinctly higher, and
the school teaching of History (though it still varies
widely in different schools) is on the whole far more
intelligent and scientific than it was when the examination began. Whatever opinions may be held as

to the higher part of the Board examinations, it will generally be admitted that they have done much to raise the minimum standard of requirement.

After these preliminary remarks on the history and policy of the Higher Certificate Examination, I go on to discuss its working as at present arranged, and to suggest how it may best be used by the public schools so as to secure the ends which the schools and the Board have in common : (1) the maintenance of efficient elementary teaching ; (2) the promotion of higher studies.

And first as to the general arrangement of the examination and of the subjects composing it. The certificate is not granted in the first instance unless a candidate passes in four subjects taken from three out of the four groups into which the examination is divided (i. Languages, ii. Mathematics, iii. Scripture Knowledge, English, and History, iv. Natural Science), or in three languages and either Mathematics or Natural Science. But a boy who has already gained a certificate, if he chooses to become a candidate for a second time, is allowed greater freedom, and may limit himself to any two groups. This arrangement seems a reasonable reconciliation of the principles of general education and elasticity of studies which schools and schoolmasters should have in view, and it will to some degree determine the lines on which the examination may be most conveniently used. Most schools will find it convenient to send in their boys as early as possible for the subjects required by the Universities. Those boys who are old enough to be allowed to specialize would then be able to devote most of their time to their special study without having the fear of Responsions or the Previous Examination before their eyes. Unfortunately many schoolmasters adopt the converse method. They take a boy from his general studies too early (say at the fifth form), set him at special work in Mathematics or Natural Science, and then cram him at the last moment before he leaves school with the modicum of Latin and Greek which they think will carry him into the University. Supposing however that the course above suggested is followed, the successful candidate entering for examination a second time will naturally take some of his old subjects with a view to gaining distinction in them, and combine with them one or more subjects which he has not taken before. He may, for instance, seek distinction in Latin and Greek and a Pass in History or a Modern Language, while if he is on the Modern Side he will naturally take a new Modern Language or a branch of Natural Science.

Thus one might suggest as typical specimens of two years of the examination :—

    1. Classical Side :—

        First year. Latin, Greek, Elementary Mathematics, French (or Scripture).

        Second year. Latin and Greek (for distinction), Scripture (or French), History.

2. Modern Side :—

First year. Latin, Greek, Elementary Mathematics, French (or Scripture or Chemistry).

Second year. French (for distinction), German, English, History ;

or, Elementary and Additional Mathematics (for distinction), German, Chemistry, Physics.

These are given merely as specimens of the way in which the examination may be adjusted to the demands of general and special education respectively.

Another policy is, however, possible. In many schools it would be better for boys who have already obtained certificates to be examined by means of special and higher papers, instead of being sent in year after year for the Certificate Examination. But this is difficult to carry out in smaller schools, on account both of expense and of the arrangement of classes. With regard to expense, it may be well to remind the schools concerned that, if they are content to wait for marks till the end of August, the cost of the Higher Certificate Examination is limited to the fees of the candidates. On the same condition the cost of the General Papers for Lower Forms (see Regulations, pp. 35, 36) is also considerably reduced. If schools were ready to save money in this way, they would have more to spend on examinations, oral or written, specially suited to their own work and curriculum.

For it must not be forgotten that the work of the

Board is not limited to the Certificate Examination. It also examines and inspects schools of the highest grade, either as a whole or in part, in any subjects of school teaching. It is true that many schools on the score of expense confine themselves to the Certificate Examination, where the chief cost falls on the candidate ; but it is very desirable that every school that can afford it should have some part of its examination specially adapted to its particular needs, by having either papers specially composed for it, or an oral examination or inspection of some part of the work by an experienced examiner. Either process would secure at once greater freedom for the examiner and a fuller test of the higher teaching of the schools.

The scheme proposed above for examinations of two successive years no doubt implies a considerable advance upon the present standard of school work ; but the performance of certain schools shows that it is not beyond the powers of teachers or boys. Of course the examination is purposely arranged to suit almost any succession or combination of the subjects generally studied in schools of the higher grade, but the scheme suggested has the great advantage of keeping the boys together until their education has really reached a stage at which specialization becomes profitable.

The exact point in a school at which a boy ought to be able to take the Pass papers in each subject will depend on the size of the school and the arrangement of the classes. But it may be said generally that the boys in a lower Sixth Form ought to be able to pass in the Latin and Greek and Mathematical papers. Several schools indeed send in still lower forms; but at least the standard suggested should not imply any strain on ordinary resources. In an average lower Sixth the boys will have been learning Latin and Mathematics for at least five or six years, and Greek for at least three or four. If the teaching is what it should be, the boys will have had plenty of practice before them in Unprepared Translations in both the languages. Greek Prose, it will be borne in mind, is not a compulsory subject for a 'Pass'; its place may be taken by a Greek prepared book. Latin Prose, on the other hand, is a necessary sub-ject, but the standard is not higher than may be fairly expected from boys who have been learning Latin for five or six years. Indeed only the in-grained habit of expecting little of the public school boy could make the certificate standard in Latin and Greek appear unduly severe. The concession by which exemption from Responsions is granted to candidates who satisfy the examiners in the bare equivalent (see above, p. 263) has removed the com-plaint that the examination is not adjusted to the corresponding standard set in the University; but happily only a comparatively small proportion of boys enter the University by means of this inferior avenue. The large majority of those who obtain exemption by means of this examination do so by gaining a full certificate, i. e. by satisfying the examiners in Latin, Greek, Elementary Mathematics, and a fourth subject[1]. If a boy has once gained a certificate including Latin and Greek, he will be able in subsequent years, according to the new regulations which came into force in 1898, to dispense with the Pass papers in Latin Prose and in Latin and Greek Unprepared Translation, and to concentrate his attention on the higher papers in these subjects. No doubt in some schools it will happen that in the same form will be found some boys taking the 'Pass' papers and some taking the higher, but there ought to be no great difficulty in so adjusting the marks on the two sets of papers as to do no injustice to either class of boys. The more advanced papers in Composition and Translation ought to give fair scope for the ability of an Upper Sixth boy. If further tests are needed, they may be found in the optional paper of critical questions (see Regulations for 1898, p. 35) which the Board undertakes to provide. The new arrangement must at first be experimental, but it has at least the merit of

[1] In 1897 the number of candidates who gained a certificate exempting from Responsions was 547; of those obtaining *special* exemption without a certificate 27. The Winchester 'notion' for the document granting this special exemption, 'ticket-of-leave,' happily expresses the shade of reproach attaching to it. It must be borne in mind however that many of those who obtain exempting certificates do not go to the University, and that a large number of boys never go in for the Certificate Examination, and still enter the Universities through Responsions or the Previous Examination.

attempting to combine the encouragement of higher study with the strict maintenance of a minimum 'Pass' standard.   The influence of the examination hitherto has perhaps been rather in the direction of raising the average standard of attainment ; it is to be hoped that the prominence now given to the more advanced work may serve as a stimulus to higher study in the schools concerned, and may remind Sixth Form masters that their work is not done when they have brought their boys up to the standard of the ' Pass' papers in the Certificate Examination.

The prepared books in Latin and Greek have from time to time been the subject of misunderstanding among schoolmasters.   It may be well to remind my readers that (1) a candidate for special exemption from Responsions or the Previous Examination must satisfy the examiners in a prepared book both in Greek and Latin (see p. 263) ; (2) a candidate, in order to pass in Greek for the certificate, must satisfy the examiners either in Greek Prose or in a Greek book.

With these two exceptions, books are not required of candidates in Greek or Latin, any more than they are required of candidates in French and German. The policy of the Board has been to encourage the reading of the best authors, but to make its ' Pass' and ' Distinction ' in languages depend mainly on Composition and Unprepared Translation. The books prescribed by the Board are such as may conveniently occupy the work of a Sixth Form, Upper or Lower, for one or two terms of the school year.   Schools which prefer to take other books as part of the examination can do so by Regulation 17, a clause of which advantage is frequently taken. The lists are so arranged as to suggest for reading, in rotation, most of the principal Latin and Greek classics. This part of the preparation for the Board Examination would naturally come in the terms after Christmas. According to the present arrangements, both at Oxford and at Cambridge, most of the College scholarship examinations fall in the Michaelmas Term, with the result that the form-work of this term is a good deal disturbed. The term is also much occupied in rearranging the forms and getting them into working order after the promotions following the summer examinations. For these reasons the natural time for reading the Certificate books would come later, and most schools have some examination of their own in December, which forms the fitting test of the work of the Michaelmas Term. But even in the later terms of the year, the work of a Sixth Form will of course not be confined to the books for the Certificate Examination. Wide reading is an essential element in all serious study of the classics. The Certificate books represent a minimum of requirement.

The papers for the Higher Certificate have sometimes been criticized as not affording a sufficiently searching test of the books read. The answer to this is to be found in the Higher Certificate Time-table. Unless the examination is to be made excessively burdensome, the Book papers must be confined in ordinary cases within moderate limits. At the same time the new regulations admit of special arrangements where such are desired. Some years ago the obligatory papers in Latin and Greek Grammar included a second part containing critical questions, and some schoolmasters, for whose opinions I have a great respect, regret the change by which these questions are relegated to an optional paper which does not count for a certificate. They think that this is to give too much weight to Composition, which to many boys comes as a happy gift of nature, and that the value of strict training in the scientific and historical aspects of language is thereby unduly ignored. This is a question on which the opinion of the Head-Masters' Conference and of the Head-Masters' Association would be helpful. The recent change had, I think, the approval of the majority of head-masters; but there is no doubt that the Board would carefully consider any representation made to it on the subject.

To return to the more general aspects of the Classical part of the examination. The complete range of the Classical teaching in a school cannot perhaps be fully tested in an examination which has to include a 'Pass' element, with a standard which is in definite relation to the Pass Examinations of the Universities; but, as it stands, the main and essential part of classical study is tested in the papers in Composition and Translation. A school which works on sound lines ought to be able to have its boys ready for this test at the end of the school year without any special 'cramming' or any disorganization of school studies.

Without trenching on the ground occupied by other writers, I may point out one or two matters of interest in connexion with the examination in Modern Languages. First and foremost, no one who has seen the deplorable unreadiness of the average public school boy to attack a book in French or German, still more to write a letter in either language, will doubt that somehow or other the power of reading fluently and writing correctly in these languages is still very imperfectly acquired in public schools. Some improvement has been made in schools of late years in the teaching of both languages, but, though the standard has risen, there is still great room for improvement. All boys who go in for the Higher Certificate ought at one examination or other to be able to pass in at least one of these two languages, and thereby gain exemption from the Additional Subject at Responsions and the Previous Examination, a great practical convenience for many of those who are going to the Universities. Here again, if the teaching is sound from the beginning, boys in a Lower Sixth Form ought to have no difficulty in satisfying the requirements of the Board in Grammar, Composition, and Unprepared Translation. If the language is well taught from the first, a very few hours a week in school ought to be sufficient to keep up the power of translation and composition in a Sixth Form. This takes for granted that a boy has acquired enough interest in French or German to be willing to read it on his own account, and this is not too much to expect in a school of the highest grade. There are schools still where modern languages, as well as Latin and Greek, are taught for many years without bearing fruit in any real knowledge of the language or love of the literature, but these schools, it is to be hoped, are growing rarer, and teachers are recognizing more generally that a training in language which ends in Grammar and 'Exercises' condemns itself. Whether the subject be an ancient language or a modern one, the chief available test of proper teaching must be Translation and Composition, and by these tests the class-teaching of French and German must stand or fall. No cramming dodge is necessary to face these tests with success; if a boy has been taught really to exercise his wits on the language, he will be ready to pass his examination when the time comes without any strain and without any interference with the rest of his work.

With regard to Mathematics one point in the policy of the Board has proved a stumbling-block. Just as, in order to pass in Latin and Greek, a knowledge of the elementary accidence is required, so in Mathematics a candidate is required to satisfy the examiners in the elements of Arithmetic, Euclid, and Algebra, in order to pass in the more advanced part of the subject. Whether this policy is wise or not in principle may be open to question, but it is necessary in practice in an examination which is accepted as exempting from the University Pass Examinations in these subjects. On the whole the few grievances that arise are more than outweighed by the advantage of enforcing rigid accuracy in the elements from all who are devoting much time to Mathematics.

If the view stated earlier be adopted, that a boy goes in for the Higher Certificate Examination for the first time in the Lower Sixth, he would naturally take Elementary Mathematics as one of his subjects. If he has been well taught, he ought by this time to have no difficulty in reaching the standard required. Many boys would be able at this stage to satisfy the examiners in Additional Mathematics as well. After this it is a question partly of educational principle, partly of individual taste, whether a boy should still keep up his mathematical studies, and it is a question on which probably a wide variety in practice exists in different schools. In general, most boys who have once passed in Elementary Mathematics would find little difficulty in doing so again, if they should wish to take it as one of the four subjects for obtaining a certificate.

The other subjects of the Higher Certificate Examination are those of the English group and the Natural Science group. With regard to History and to Natural Science there are special chapters in this book to which I leave the discussion of these subjects. I will say a few words on Scripture Knowledge and English. The former is, next to Classics and Mathematics, the subject most widely taken in the examination, and it is one on which there are as many opinions as masters. But probably most of those who have experience of teaching the subject will agree that the new arrangement, by which the 'Outlines' are to be taken in sections, will tend to make the subject more 'educational' and less subdued to the limits of the hand-book. As the subject now stands, a Sixth Form master, teaching boys who probably have been reading the Bible since they came to school, should have no difficulty in presenting them for this subject in the last year or the last but one before they leave. There are still 'irreconcilables' who say that the subject is not one for examination at all, but I doubt whether on the whole the ablest teachers would deny that it is possible to examine in Old and New Testament history and in the Greek text of special books of the New Testament in such a way as to encourage scientific training and literary skill without destroying or degrading the human and the spiritual interest which makes the subject so potent a means of education.

But I must leave this to the experts to discuss; all I am concerned to point out here is that the subject is one which comes well within the range of a Lower Sixth Form boy, and that he ought to be able to take it without difficulty 'in his stride.'

English, in spite of the isolated efforts of individual head-masters, can hardly be called yet a regular part of public school work, except on the Modern Side. The want of it is seen in the incapacity either to analyze a piece of difficult English or to write an original essay often shown by the average Sixth Form boy in a Matriculation Examination. But even in schools where English is not a general subject, it will probably be taught on the Modern Side, and for boys on this side it will naturally be taken up for the Certificate Examination in one year or another. Greater attention will probably be paid to the writing of essays, now that an essay is exacted from all candidates who desire complete exemption from Part II of the Previous Examination.

The tendency of modern education, many of us feel, is rather to raise the average level than to develop exceptional ability, and perhaps the most serious objection made against the Certificate Examination is that it tends to stereotype a lower minimum of knowledge than may fairly be demanded of a public school, while it gives hardly sufficient scope for boys who are above the average in reading and ability. The danger of consulting the interests of the average boy is one that has constantly to be guarded against; but, as I said at the outset, we must accept the facts, recognize that the examination represents a compromise, and do what we can to improve it from time to time within these limits. I will only add this to what I have already said :— that an examination which, with regard to Classics, lays its chief stress on Composition and Unprepared Translation, is in the right way, and that it ought to be possible to provide for higher work in them without upsetting the useful function of the ex-amination as a standard University examination for the average public school boy.

P. E. MATHESON.

SOME little time ago there was discussed at a school-boy debating society an oddly worded motion to the effect that 'too much novel-reading was undesirable.' The speakers were boys, with the sympathies of boyhood for novels, and the generous disregard of boyhood for the lore of nicely calculated less or more ; and one and all opposed the motion. A master who was present endeavoured to support it. He had, he said, no ill will to novels as such ; he was keenly alive to their many merits. But he pointed out cogently enough that the motion as worded carried itself; that it was possible to have too much even of a good thing ; and that, granting novels were good things, yet too much of them was dangerous, wasteful of time, at the least undesirable. But it was to no purpose that he spoke. Logic, persuasion, earnestness availed him nothing ; and when the division was taken he found himself alone, even the original proposer of the motion having, I believe, been converted to the other side.

It is however with the attitude of that lonely master, rather than with the cause of the strongest battalions, that the present writer would wish to identify himself, as he attempts to discuss the question of public school athletics. His position with regard to it, put simply, is this. Athletics are good, but it is possible to have too much of them ; and that is undesirable.

The question is certainly one which all who care about education are bound to take into account. For some time past people connected with the Universities and the Public Schools have been asking themselves whether athleticism has not been developing into something like a tyranny, and the worship of athletics into an idolatry. And this last summer a popular discussion on the whole subject was raised in the *Times* over such a highly unimportant detail as the duration of the Eton and Harrow match. Those actually engaged in teaching are touched more nearly ; to them it is not so much a matter of theory as a problem affecting their own attitude and example. They need not discuss it or commit themselves verbally to any position regarding it ; but their practice causes them somehow to be popularly ranged in one or other of two opposed camps, the extreme sections of which may be represented on the one side by the common belief that all that is manliest and best and most encouraging in the English public school system revolves around, if it is not dependent upon, athletics, and on the other by the dictum of a well-known educationalist, 'To me these athletics are the devil.'

It would serve little practical purpose to argue at length about the abstract value of our athletics. They are there, and we have just to make the best use of them we can. Moreover, up to a certain point almost every one is agreed. A schoolmaster would be ungrateful indeed who did not respect them. There is no question, I think, that the spread of athletics and the better organization of games have tended to enlist the boys' sympathies on the side of law. Therein also is found the greatest help towards the solution of the problem of dealing with boys in the mass; for so all kinds of different temperaments, the keen and the dreamy, the gregarious and the unsociable, the 'limb' and the lounger, are swept along on the tide of one universal interest quite social and wholesome in tone.

Then, as regards the effect on the boys' characters, if the object of education be the training of character, no one can doubt that, for English lads at any rate, towards that training athletics furnish a salutary, potent, and necessary contribution. We need not repeat again all that has been so often urged about the dependence of the healthy mind upon the healthy body, about the necessity of recreation and the manliness engendered by such recreation as English boys are accustomed to take; the strength, courage, good temper that athletics both demand and supply; the value of the discipline they enforce; the unselfishness that is learnt in working for one's side rather than for oneself; the training to face responsibilities and go through ordeals; how the young athlete carries the hopes and the honour of his school or house upon his shoulders, and learns in the process both independence and *savoir faire*, and along with these a certain adaptability of character which will make him hereafter capable of mingling with all sorts and conditions of men, without shyness on the one hand or presumption on the other.

Life-lessons these, that are being taught, and in the immediate present our athletics give us two other and particular blessings, for which we should be properly thankful. One of these is that they supply a subject of thought and conversation that is perfectly legitimate, perfectly wholesome, and within limits not unprofitable. Boys at school pass through a period of life during which bodies and minds are rapidly growing, interests are being developed, and prospects of new pleasures and activities are opening out. And it is much that during such a period, when dangers and perversions of energy are nigh at hand, there should be one master interest, healthy and absorbing, to dominate speech and thought. That is one great consideration. And another, not indeed so important but still of very great importance, is this. The system of to-day is closely bound up with the maintenance of intimate and friendly relations between teacher and taught, between master and boy. But for the maintenance of such relations there is needed some neutral ground, not connected with the extraction of work or the giving and receiving of moral harangues, on which the two parties may meet and fraternize. And in athletics just such a neutral ground is provided.

Thus it would be absurd to try to get rid of the athletic element. In truth the time has long passed for decision between a simple Yes or No; the real point at issue now is the far subtler and more delicate question of Less or More.

Now it is certain that the present century has seen, we will not say the rise of athletics *ab ovo*, but the discovery of their possibilities as an educational instrument. The enthusiasm for active exercise is indeed no new thing. From time immemorial the English have been passionately fond of sports and pastimes. Our boys are born with the athletic spirit inherited from their forefathers; and the fact that the English system of education has allowed it more or less free scope is what chiefly distinguishes our schools from those on the Continent. The healthiness of our games, the liberty, the chastening discipline, are said to be the envy of foreigners no less than the pride of ourselves. 'Great heavens!' such is the exclamation Mr. Geoffrey Drage puts into the mouths of non-English parents as they look upon the faces of English lads, 'Great heavens, why are not our boys like that?' We who are borne on the full flood of the athletic sea may permit ourselves the luxury of gazing back for a moment on the shores from which we have come, the small beginnings

that have led us so surely to great endings. Take
Eton for instance, and contrast the situation described
in 'Eton of old, or Eighty years since,' with the state
of things to-day. Then games were still in their
infancy; recognized, indeed, but not as yet established. For exercise the many were dependent on
bathing and boating in the summer, on hoops apparently for the rest of the year; the few played cricket
and football. There were in existence three cricket
clubs, having, I imagine, regular games and playing
two or three foreign matches a year. No cricket, or
for the matter of that no football, was ever played on
whole school-days. At football there was practically
only one game, the wall game, at which eighteen or
twenty played on each side, every one who came
down being chosen in. Only a small minority, it
is obvious, and that composed mostly of the same
boys, can have taken part in these exercises. There
were no beagles. Compulsory football was of course
unknown. If you wished to play, you played; if not,
you might do something else. The something else
might take the form of fives; but there was only
one court, that which was formed by the projecting
buttresses of the chapel, and few can have taken
advantage of the opportunity it gave. On the whole
it is clear that what games there were were mostly
informal and unorganized. The authorities said,
'There are the playing-fields; they are your own;
make the best of them, for we give you absolutely
nothing else. Yes, we concede to you the interval

between three chapel buttresses; you may play fives in them.'

This was in the first two decades of the century. And now there are fifty fives courts where before there was one; twenty games or thereabouts of cricket as against three; compulsory football for every house four or five times a week; to say nothing of beagles and athletic sports in the Easter Term, and rowing and bathing daily through the summer. There are house colours for football and school colours for football, cricket, rowing, racquets; there are challenge cups, senior and junior, the records of victorious merit.

What is true of Eton is, I believe, true, *mutatis mutandis*, of the other great public schools; the comprehensive net of athletics has closed around them all, sweeping in our boys by shoals, and few are the puny minnows that swim through its meshes. And yet the whole system is entirely modern; most of it a development of the last forty years. I suppose it is from Dr. Arnold that we may date the beginning of this new era. He was, it is said, the first headmaster who ever looked on at a game. Till his time the authorities one and all held rigidly aloof from any interference with the boys at their play; with him there arose a generation of masters who aimed at being friends and companions as well as task-masters. Once it was seen that you could command the respect and affection of lads by becoming in some sort a boy yourself, the way was opened for that magisterial encouragement of athleticism which has since borne such abundant fruit. Thenceforth it was the master who raised funds for new fives courts, new cricket grounds; he who instructed and 'coached'; he who was fain to encourage the organization of games, and to rearrange the time-tables of work with that design. It was inevitable that this change of attitude on the part of the authorities, synchronizing with a very general development of the athletic spirit in the country at large, should produce wide-reaching results among the boys. They were eager to accept the altered situation; for new facilities meant the awakening of new interest in a field already so congenial. Athletics ceased to be a pastime, and became a sacred institution, on which scholastic hands must not be profanely laid. The result on the boys is something like this. A public opinion—I am speaking generally, and disregarding for the present particular exceptions—has sprung up which causes the majority of boys to believe nothing in the world comparable to athletic prowess. Parliaments come and go; empires totter to their fall; but they are intent on the result of the latest house match, and drinking in each morning the contents of the *Sportsman.* They are hero-worshippers of course, but who are their heroes? Not the scholars, not the Sixth Form, not the masters, but the athlete who represents the school at cricket or football. He is privileged in a sense in which no monitor is ever privileged. He claims, and the claim is unresistingly admitted by his fellows as valid, the liberties and the homage that belong to the great ones, the natural leaders of men. He and those like him form a close oligarchy, who give the tone to the rest. And it is on his athletics that his position rests. All other facts with regard to him are of secondary importance. He does his work, or he does it not, but the popular estimate of him is not affected one way or another by his performance there. What he reads, what he cares about outside his games are just so many diversions, distinct from the main business of his life, which is to be athletically great. But because he is that, his words are as oracles, himself the admirable Crichton, in whose place every ambitious junior hopes one day to be[1]. Some day he may care about political and social questions, and the like; then it will perhaps be his province to settle them, not because he has made them specially his own, but because he is a Carlylese hero, the born prophet and king, no Mahomet who must painfully go to the mountain, but a transcendent being to whom mountains come. For the present therefore his athletics are all-absorbing; for the future, if he lets himself forecast it, they seem by no means indifferent.

Nor is he wholly wrong. There is enough of truth

[1] 'A cricketer,' so says the Jubilee book on cricket, ' is just a man with a clear eye, bronzed face, and athletic figure. He is usually somewhat lacking in general information' (let us note that in passing) 'and is sometimes a poor conversationalist upon any but his own subject; he does not read much.'

in the prevalent schoolboy idea that to be athletic ensures at least a probability of a good professional berth in after-life to make it a factor of the situation. So our young hero feels pretty certain that his athletic prominence of to-day will stand him in good stead then. 'I shall try to get into the army,' says he to himself, 'probably through the militia. If I fail, I shall look out for a mastership somewhere. You can get lots of holidays, lots of cricket and football then.'

Such, still speaking generally, is the conventional attitude. It may not be ideally the right attitude, but for the present it holds the field. And if it be the best of which boys in the main are capable, we, like Solon, may as well legislate accordingly, and identify ourselves with the athletic movement. So far the outward results of that movement seem eminently reassuring. Certainly the prominent boys can now be depended upon, as a rule, to uphold rather than undermine authority. Certainly, too, through games our boy-athletes acquire a way with them such as, to be quite honest, the average boy-student often fails to attain. Contrast the bright, cheery, unintellectual conversation of the athlete at a master's breakfast-table with the dull, flat pointlessness of the nervous and silent student, and you find yourself wondering involuntarily, as you look on this picture and on that, whether the received opinion is not after all right, and the old chilly idea of the superiority of mind over matter untenable.

And yet these and the like considerations are not strictly relevant. No one proposes now to destroy, or even to relegate to an obscure position, the part of athletics. All that is required is to set them in their proper place, and then see that they encroach no further. Perhaps we shall do this best by turning now from the credit to the debit side of the account. Let us consider the price we have to pay for what athletics give us.

Something might be said under the literal heading of costliness. Of course the organization of athletics has involved a great deal of expense—expense in connexion with the plant, with the salaries of ground men and professionals, with personal and general outfit. Any school that would recommend itself to the British public must concern itself to see that its athletic appliances do not fall behind its neighbours'. There is a very keen competition, more especially among the private schools, and for his own part the writer is inclined to think that it has gone too far. Without at all sighing for the rougher wickets, the straitened playground, the voluntary system, he yet regrets the excess of expenditure which the new regime seems to involve. And this, firstly, because there is, he thinks, too much athletic coddling. At private schools little boys become too fastidious; they never learn to contend against difficulties. Secondly, because as a result boys' ideas are on too magnificent a scale. They see that the authorities spare no expense, and they themselves come to think that no expense should be spared. And, thirdly, because athletics on the whole are very well able to look after themselves. The boys already over-estimate their importance ; they ought not to be encouraged so to do from the example of their instructors.

Then there is the question of the time given to athletics. I suppose different schools vary very much in this respect from one another; but I do not know of any public school of which it could be said now that too little time is given to games; and certainly there are many against which the complaint is raised that they give too much. They most of them have their three half-holidays a week, and on whole school-days a solid space of two hours (perhaps two such spaces) left clear for play. Surely the time thus provided is enough; if on half-holidays the whole afternoon is sacred to play, then the morning should be sacred to work, and any encroachments there on the part of athletics should be firmly dis-couraged. At least, if there be such encroachment, it should be for the younger not the older boys. Dr. Clement Dukes, who is a leading authority on school hygiene, gives a table of scales of work during school life. He thinks that boys of twelve to fourteen should work twenty-five hours a week, boys of eighteen to nineteen should work fifty. Some public schools seem to be inverting this proportion. There is another encroachment which must be resisted. We need not grudge the hours given to exercise in which a boy is himself actively participating, but we do need to restrict the time that is devoted merely to watching the play of others. It is an innocent occupation enough, for a short period; but what a pitiful waste of opportunity are those long summer days of which most of the morning and the whole of the afternoon are devoted to 'looking on'! Once more, lest we should think conversation about athletics adequate to all our needs, let us hear the reflection of a distinguished man on the defects of his youth. 'What I regret now,' said he, 'is the time I spent as a boy not on playing games, but on talking about them.'

But on the whole it is not the time occupied that constitutes the greatest difficulty. That could in most respects be reduced to reasonable limits by judicious legislation. What really dismays thinking men (who are not necessarily non-athletic men) is a more intangible thing—I mean the attitude of public opinion on the subject. That schoolboy conviction of which I have already spoken and which nothing seems likely to shake, namely, that athletics are the one thing in the world worth caring about, tends to thrust all other interests into the shade. It is not that other subjects do not appeal. Talk to boys individually, and you shall find no lack of embryo enthusiasm; this one is keen about pictures, that one about moths, or steam-engines, or heraldry, or what not. But such individual interests and hobbies never come to the light. They blush unseen, if they do not languish and die, during the period of a boy's public-school career: the system as a whole has no use for them; it gives them no recognition, no encouragement.

Or take the case of matters more strictly intellectual. It is not that boys leave school knowing less than they used; on the whole they do more hours of work, and a stricter tale of bricks is demanded of them now. But they go through their calendar of working days without in most cases ever having the divine thirst for knowledge stimulated, and some who came with it lose the love they had. This is not a natural process. The natural thing is for boys to like all work that is not lessons, and even as to lessons, if they are indifferent about the matter of them, to be keenly interested in the tangible results. Surely more might be made of material that is so promising. Athletics should not monopolize the room; it should not be the case that, when the work is done, it is done perfunctorily, with thoughts otherwise, 'in the field, by the fold.'

One must not expect enthusiasm from the many; one may be prepared for inertness. But the heart-breaking thing is to find in so many cases no consciousness of loss, to see the little fellow's early enthusiasm fade into indifference, and finally perish through atrophy, as he comes to think that all knowledge taught at school is useless. 'What is the good of it?' he asks. 'When I leave, I shall never open a book.' 'Athletics,' said an excellent boy to me the other day, 'are much more useful than classics at the University; they get you into lots of colleges there.'

Is it natural that under such auspices scholarship should flourish? At least it is a fact full of significance that the great percentage of intellectual prizes at the Universities are no longer won by the schools most conspicuous for athletics. Of course these turn out their scholars still; but the fact remains that in spite of a better organized system of work, in spite of earnest and scholarly-minded masters who really care about intellectual matters and who might fairly hope to impress their convictions on the boys, the boarding schools with their cult of athletics, judged by the standard of University successes, fall far behind the less athletic day schools.

Once again, the supremacy of athletics involves a danger on the moral side. In the midst of their fascination it is terribly easy to forget that, though good in themselves, they are not goodness; no, nor an equivalent for goodness. Recognize as much as you please how much healthy physical conditions conduce to a general healthy tone; yet the fact remains that these may coexist with a great deal of moral evil. It is sometimes seen how, when an athlete of coarser fibre strays into high places, he is accepted and tolerated by his fellows, who may even for a time appear to take their tone collectively from him—not because they really approve of him, but because his athleticism is thought to constitute a claim which other considerations may not override. Then the falseness of the athletic ideal stands self-convicted.

Some distinctions however must be made. There are boys whose inclinations are naturally intellectual rather than athletic, and who may remain uninfluenced by the prevailing tone of thought. There are others, neither intellectual nor athletic, who are distinguished by unusual independence of character. Such boys go their own way. But in both these cases the system acts prejudicially. The former are not felt; the latter are not liked. Both are in some sense outside the general life of the school; they do not contribute as much as they ought to the general well-being, they do not get much out of the school themselves. Though they stand really on a higher plane than the mere athlete, they receive little public recognition, and in their isolation become exclusive, or—shall we say it ?—priggish. They suffer under the pressure of a public opinion that has another ideal than their own. And the leaders of that public opinion, the athletes themselves, it is foolish to pretend that they do not suffer. Some of them, it is true, escape the spell, and consistently hold a right sense of proportion, developing the *mens sana* alongside of the *corpus sanum*. But such are on the whole the exceptions, and we are not speaking of them. Of the majority we fear it may truly be said that, however muscular and sturdy they become, they are sadly limited in scope. They are lacking in ideas, and that must tell eventually. They may be leaders of boyhood now, but they will not be leaders of men hereafter, at least not the best sort of leaders. When they have done with school and University, their sun begins to set. The time must come when for mere social effectiveness they will need a wider horizon. They will mix with educated men ; they will hear political, literary, social questions discussed, and then they will come to feel the unsatisfactoriness of being unable to take their part in rational or intellectual conversation. They cannot be athletic for ever ; and when their athletic powers fail, there must be regrets that in their youth matter had the preference over mind. Or, if not, what shall we hope for their old age—long days spent in cricket pavilions, varied by large doses of golf and endless chatter about old athletic days ; for occupation, the compiling of others' averages, and for reading, the literature of sport ?

That there is then at school a tyranny of athletics and an idolatry of athletics, the writer believes. In what direction safeguards , may be found is more difficult to say. Yet there are one or two classes of persons who might help to provide them, and to them an appeal may fairly be made.

First, the head-masters. They if they will can do much. They can, by legislation, by stern repression of inroads upon the work, by refusing to over-advertize their schools with athletic displays, by selecting their assistant-masters for other qualifications than mere athleticism, regulate the tendency to waste, and induce a more rational public opinion on the subject. Theirs is the directest and most effective agency for attacking the evil. However, the point is so obvious that it may seem superfluous to dwell upon it.

Then next, the parents. They are primarily concerned to secure that their boys should turn out complete men. They too, and no one else to the same extent, are responsible for what their boys are to be. They then, if age and experience can teach at all, should know already what their sons have slowly to learn, that physical development is only one form of growth, and that it is essentially a lower form than either intellectual or moral growth.

But do they know it? In many cases the parents are more boyish than the boys themselves. What schoolmaster is not familiar with such parental aspirations as this? 'I do not want my boy to be a scholar, but I do want him to join to the full in the active life of the place. I believe the boys who turn out best in the long run are not your bookworms, but the fellows who play their games heartily: I was never much of a hand at books myself. Make the boy a man and not a nonentity. He ought to be a cricketer: indeed I have had a professional to coach him in the holidays[1].'

[1] I cannot refrain from quoting in this place the story told by Mr. A. H. Gilkes in the *National Review* for September,

That is it. The boy is to cultivate athletics at school; and, as if that were not enough, the holidays too are mapped out with a view to secure the maximum of athletic exercise and the minimum of everything else. He takes few walks, except to shoot; he has little ear for the voices of birds, and little eye for scenery; does not distinguish between different trees and flowers; reads no poetry, visits no picture galleries. Nor does it stop there. Cases are known where a father has sacrificed his boy's prospects of getting into Sandhurst, because an extra year at school may offer an uncertain chance of getting into the Eleven. An instance is quoted where a doctor's report that a boy's heart was too weak to allow of his rowing in the Eton Eight was overridden by a hasty telegram from home. These may be exceptional cases, but they are not an uncommon type. They are frequent enough to justify the question to parents whether this exclusive

1897. ' I was lately dining,' he says, ' in the company of a gentleman, a parent, who after dinner said to me with some feeling in his tone, that he had that day taken his son to ——, naming a great school, and that he had taken the opportunity given him by the parting to give his boy the best advice in his power. I said that the occasion was well chosen, for that when a boy was going into a strange and perilous life he needed guidance; and, moreover, that then his heart was soft and open, and then he would receive and remember what he said. The father agreed with me, and said that the advice which he had given his boy was to take up bowling rather than batting, as likely really to be of more service to him. *Quid dicam, hac senectute ?* '

athleticism is what they mean when they talk of giving their boys a liberal education. No one wishes them to be indifferent to their boys' athletic interests; that would merely mean alienating their sympathies. But things must be kept in their true proportion ; the son must see that his father at any rate looks beyond immediate successes to ultimate effects on character and life; that he regards athletics as not an end in themselves, but only at best a means to an end. Unless English parents will make that clear, it is vain to hope that their children at school will rise above the conventional standard of inconsiderate athletic-worship.

And lastly, what of the race of schoolmasters themselves ? They can do something, but not everything. Boys do not always reverence their instructors. They are capable of hearing appeals with deaf ears, of remaining unconvinced by the most cogent arguments addressed to their reason. A man who is a schoolmaster must be content to find his best endeavours frustrated by a quiet and polite but perfectly firm resistance. Still, he has certain advantages which no one else can have; he is on the spot, for one thing; his jurisdiction when he speaks officially is unquestioned, for another. If he is himself a good athlete, his words will carry additional weight, and certainly his personal example will tell. On the whole, if he can do nothing, probably no one else will. Therefore the last appeal must be to him.

But when you come to meet the schoolmaster, you

must be prepared to find him not wholly on your side. For the schoolmaster of to-day is no mere pedagogue with academic mind and furrowed brow; or, as Charles Lamb describes him, 'boy-rid, worn out with perpetual boy.' He is a warm creature of flesh and blood, who loves his exercise himself and has even to fight temptation in regard thereto. It is well known how desirous the private schools are of securing for masters men who have distinguished themselves athletically at the Universities. Something of the same kind is true, though in a less degree, of the public schools. The old requirement of a first-class degree, though not wholly done away with, is nevertheless modified in a number of particular instances. One man at least, and sometimes more than one, whose duty shall be to look after the games, is felt to be required at each place. There is no doubt much to be said for such accommodations. I suppose that at private schools the main requisite in a master is that he should be genial and boylike and stimulating, with a wholesome clean mind; and the combination of qualities is perhaps easiest found among athletes. But for older boys and public school life, something more is desirable—a wider outlook, imagination, ideals; and the athletic man has these qualities, not by grace, but by cultivation. He starts with a great advantage; the boys look up to him and admire him as one of themselves; the possibilities of his personal influence are great. But he must see to it that he possesses something more

than a stone to give when the cry is for bread. Such
a man then must impose checks upon himself. If he
is wise, he will devote some part of every holiday to
self-improvement in other than athletic fields; and
while at school he will set before himself a very
rigorous standard of duty in regard to his actual
teaching : he will acknowledge higher claims upon
him than his games ; he will be prepared to sacrifice
the latter when those claims intervene. He will do
well to read sporting papers and magazines sparingly.
In his intercourse with the boys, in his breakfast and
dinner parties, he will not be content if he cannot
now and again lead the conversation to other topics
besides cricket and football. And when he speaks of
these latter, as of course he often must and will, he
will instinctively try to prevent the talk from settling
on the lees : I mean he will turn rigorously away
from the lower aspects of this kind of talk, such as
the statistical details, the 'hard luck,' the grumblings
at umpires' wrong decisions, the excuses for personal
ill-success, and draw attention to broader aspects of
things, such as good generalship, tact, good temper,
unselfishness, perseverance in an uphill struggle, and
the like. Nor is it incompatible with the utmost
keenness that he should let it be seen he too regards
games as a means only, not as an end. Of course
there is a danger of being unnatural, of talking as it
were on stilts. No one would recommend that ; but
the real point is this, that a man who professes to
educate the young ought to see things in this light,

and if he is a conscientious man he will discipline himself till he do so.

What we have to fear to-day is far more lest our masters should let themselves by their sympathy with boys be dragged down to the lower plane, than the old mistake of holding aloof and becoming out of touch with younger minds. We seem to have learnt the lesson that boys can most easily be approached through their athletics. We have to see to it now lest we forget that that is only a preliminary step, worthless unless it leads to something else; that the God who gave them bodies gave them also minds and souls; that in the Divine order soul comes first, mind second, and body last; and that though we may somewhere reach the spiritual and intellectual faculties through the physical, yet there are ever depths which the athletic plummet fails to sound.

LIONEL FORD.

OXFORD
PRINTED AT THE CLARENDON PRESS
BY HORACE HART, M.A.
PRINTER TO THE UNIVERSITY